SpringerBriefs in Information Systems

Series editor
Jörg Becker

More information about this series at http://www.springer.com/series/10189

.

Denis Trček

Trust and Reputation Management Systems

An e-Business Perspective

 Springer

Denis Trček
Faculty of Computer and Information
    Science
University of Ljubljana
Ljubljana, Slovenia, EU

ISSN 2192-4929   ISSN 2192-4937   (electronic)
SpringerBriefs in Information Systems
ISBN 978-3-319-62373-3   ISBN 978-3-319-62374-0   (eBook)
DOI 10.1007/978-3-319-62374-0

Library of Congress Control Number: 2017947495

Printed on acid-free paper

This Springer imprint is published by Springer Nature
The registered company is Springer International Publishing AG
The registered company address is: Gewerbestrasse 11, 6330 Cham, Switzerland

This book is dedicated to Tamara, Gašper, and Anže. They make my life a joy.

Preface

The changing landscape of today's business environments is notably due to extensive proliferation of digital communication technologies, where (online) trust and reputation management becomes another important issue. Why so? Trust at its core is a result of human reasoning and judgment processes. However, the environments that we humans are (evolutionary) used to deal with are being increasingly replaced by a whole new kind of environments, e-environments. And here traditional pieces of information are missing, are altered, or are present in another form. Further, permanent changes in these environments are becoming almost a norm and require rapid adaptation. And the required rate of adaptation affects not only our personal lives but increasingly so organizations, where this rate of change exceeds those that were anticipated only some 10 years ago. Put another way—current e-environments require adaptation rates that often exceed evolutionary rates of human adaptation while enforcing new behavioral patterns and providing signals that differ from traditional environments.

Evolution is a long-term process, not a matter of few decades, so nothing can be radically changed in humans, including trust that still remains one key ingredient of numerous interactions, including business interactions. And in order to help humans to deal with this new situation, computational trust and reputation management systems are being developed. These advanced technological solutions are becoming a kind of an infrastructure in the digital space that enables individuals and organizations to effectively care about their reputation while having tools that support these very individuals and organizations to more successfully evaluate the reputation of other entities and accordingly decide on trust they can attribute to them.

And this is the point where the contribution of this book comes in. Based on over 15 years of experience in the field, the book provides insights into the core pillars of trust and reputation phenomena, their management with computational systems, and how to implement these systems in business environments. Computational trust and reputation management systems are still rather evolving, being a matter of intensive research. Therefore this book provides readers with the state of the art in this field, including research, piloting, and operational implementations. Further, by taking into account anticipated trends, the materials in this book should support organizations when judging the implementation paths and investment plans to have such systems implemented timely while properly complementing their existing information systems.

Ljubljana, Slovenia, EU   Denis Trček
May 19, 2017

Acknowledgments

All professional achievements are a result of theoretical and practical knowledge gathered by numerous individuals over many generations. We all stand on someone's shoulders, and such is also the case with this book.

So, while thanks should really go to a great many individuals, excuse me for only mentioning those whose direct or indirect support was crucial to the realization of this book. They will be given in alphabetical order of their surnames:

Prof. Dr. Jose Julio Cabeza Gonzalez, Prof. Dr. Carlos Ivan Chesñevar, Prof. Dr. Gabi Dreo Rodošek, Prof. Dr. Heinz-Gerd Hegering, Prof. Dr. Günther Hödl, Prof. Dr. Gorazd Kandus, Prof. Dr. Leonid Kazovsky, Dr. Janez Korenini, Prof. Dr. Nikola Pavešić, Prof. Dr. Franc Solina, Mrs. Charlotte Taft, and Prof. Dr. Vito Turk.

Among institutions, many thanks go to my main employer, the Faculty of Computer and Information Science, University of Ljubljana, and the (current and former) members of the Laboratory of e-Media: Asst. Prof. Dr. Mira Trebar; David Jelenc, Ph.D.; Aleks Huč, M.Sc.; Iztok Starc, M.Sc.; Damjan Kovač, Ph.D.; and Eva Zupančič, Ph.D. Thanks also to my former employer, the "Jožef Stefan" Institute, where core endeavors carried out in this area some 15 years ago paved the way for this book.

Special thanks go to the people at Springer-Verlag, particularly Christian Rauscher (and also Dr. Martina Bihn). This book is yet another in the series of collaborative projects with Springer, who is a synonym for a publisher with a strong reputation, while its people are such kind of professionals that one always wants to collaborate with.

Among organizations that have provided financial support, the Slovenian Research Agency should be mentioned, in particular its funding of the research program on pervasive computing and its funding of bilateral collaborations. The European Commission should also be mentioned for its funding of numerous projects ranging from COST Action Agreement Technologies (led by Prof. Dr.

Sascha Ossowski) to the very successful European FP7 project SALUS (led by Dr. Hugo Marques). Without the support of the abovementioned institutions, this monograph would probably never have seen the light of day.

Ljubljana, Slovenia, EU   Denis Trček

Contents

Chapter 1
Introduction

Fide, sed cui, vide.
(Latin saying)

Trust and reputation are essential pillars of our societies. This probably holds even more true when it comes to business reality, whether in microeconomic or macroeconomic environments, where ubiquitous dependence on e-services and e-business paradigms in general is becoming a fact. Consequently, traditional trust and reputation issues are now manifested in different forms, and are even showing new facets. No wonder the related processes are becoming more complex and a digital-reality based kind of judgement is becoming a fact.

The unquestionable importance of trust and reputation issues at individuals, organizational, and even (inter)national levels has attracted numerous philosophical, psychological, organisational, sociological, political, and other professional endeavours. It is hard to count all of them, and even to mention them only briefly requires quite an effort. But probably one of the most influential thinkers in this field is Francis Fukuyama. His study of trust in socio-economics has shown that it is the main virtue driving the prosperity of organisations and societies as a whole. Fukuyama claims that the emerging, future structure is a network structure (organization) with a high degree of trust that will give this same structure (organization) a competitive advantage. As to reputation, do we need extensive justifications of how important reputation is for an organizations goodwill, and, consequently, its market positioning?

1.1 The Need for a Book on Trust and Reputation Systems

To repeat: Trust is a result of human reasoning and judgement processes. The traditional environments that we humans are familiar with are being rapidly replaced by whole new kinds of environments where the dynamics of changes are exceeding the trends forecasted only a few years ago. This is not just affecting us on a personal

© The Author(s) 2018
D. Trček, *Trust and Reputation Management Systems*,
SpringerBriefs in Information Systems, DOI 10.1007/978-3-319-62374-0_1

level, but also organizations are now functioning in environments that challenge their abilities of adaptation, suppress certain signals that used to be commonly available, while providing new signals that are often hard to link to traditional ones. On top of this (and because of this), adopting radically new behavioural patterns is becoming the norm.

In order to help humans and organisations to deal with this new situation, trust and reputation management systems are being developed and put into operation. These advanced systems are starting to serve as an infrastructure in digital space that enables organizations (and individuals) to better deal with trust and reputation issues. These issues range from improved evaluations of other entities' reputations to decisions about the trust that can be placed in other entities.

An interdisciplinary book such as this one is needed in order to bring together an understanding of the core pillars of trust and reputation, the roles of computational trust and reputation management systems, and their implementations in business environments (i.e. organizations in general). The book is positioned at the edges of the respective areas, and takes into account the fact that this field is still evolving. Therefore it also provides readers with insights into future trends in this area. By doing so the book should help make planning and implementation of these methods easier, while complementing existing information systems within organizations.

1.2   The Approach of This Book

In line with the above aims, the book is structured as follows. The first chapter presents the scope and the methodology that this book is based upon and identifies the targeted audience. In the second section, trust and reputation phenomena are evaluated from the perspectives of various domains, while being streamlined towards their deployment in e-business settings, which will be covered in latter sections. In the third chapter the main existing computational trust and reputation management methods and models are presented. These are evaluated in a way that tries to minimize mathematical details. In cases where such details are provided, the supporting text should be sufficient to enable a non-technical reader to get through these parts without having to delve into the given equations, while still being able to understand the core content. In the fourth section, the technological tools are given that are needed to implement computational trust and management solutions. Again, overly technical details are avoided as much as possible, but where given, the supporting text should enable non-technical readers to understand the core elements. This section also wraps-up all the previous chapters, and links them to integration steps with existing information systems as a kind of roadmap. In the fifth chapter the anticipated uses of trust and reputation management technologies are covered, while conclusions are given in the sixth chapter .

The structure and the style of the book are aligned with the target audience. The primary target audience is the top-down thinking population in organisations: the strategic and tactical level professionals like chief information officers, information

Fig. 1.1 The book methodology—a top-down approach complemented by a bottom-up approach to addressing the complementary target audiences

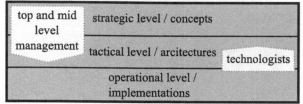

TRUST AND REPUTATION SYSTEMS

Fig. 1.2 The main domains that are covered by this book

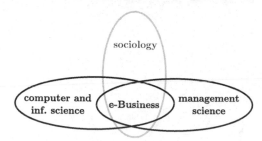

systems developers, enterprise systems architects, and so on. The secondary target audience is the higher layer of those that are dealing mainly with technological issues, but who are bottom-up oriented, such as application designers, development team leaders, product managers and so on. The interleaving of these populations across strategic, tactical and operational levels from the perspective of this book is given in Fig. 1.1. As to organisations, they are considered in the widest sense of the word, from commercial to governmental and non-profit organisations. Indeed, are there any successful and prosperous organisations where trust and reputation issues are not playing crucial roles? Further, as to domains covered, these include computer and information science, management science (and sociology in a broader sense) at the intersection of e-Business (see Fig. 1.2).

Last but not-least, the book should also be beneficial for researchers and other non-industry engaged persons who are not from the computer and information sciences, but want to get familiar with this interesting area. Hopefully it will provide them with a good starting point, because the book encompasses over 15 years of accumulated research and practical experience in this area, so the topics are presented in a concise and systematic way, with an appropriate level of historical perspective.

*   *   *

Security is one thing that is high on the agenda of any individual and society since it provides a better outlook for survival. In e-environments security is traditionally provided by solutions that are mainly based on cryptography. This kind of security is also referred to as *hard security*. Trust and reputation, on the other hand, are considered to be *soft security*. Although soft, treating them as hard as possible is a challenge, but worth the investment. The role of soft security provisioning is not inferior to traditional hard security approaches. Rather, soft security can complement traditional hard security approaches.

Chapter 2
A Brief Overview of Trust and Reputation over Various Domains

Love all, trust a few, do wrong to none.
(William Shakespeare)

The research, development and commercial efforts in trust and reputation related methods and technologies have resulted in a plethora of proposals and solutions during the past few decades—and their number is still growing. In parallel, and rather independently, trust and reputation research has also been proceeding in non-technical domains like philosophy and the social sciences. Therefore it comes as no surprise that trust and reputation have different meanings across the various domains. Consequently, being basically familiar with these variations is important if computational trust and reputation management solutions are to fulfil their mission.

More precisely, providing insights from various domains is vital to understanding these phenomena. Such approach then allows one to clearly identify which facet of trust and reputation the computational solution is going to address and why. This will also help decision makers make better decisions for their organizations based on their particular needs in terms of trust and reputation.

The above stated line of reasoning is also reflected in the aims and the structure of this chapter. We begin by covering trust in the area of philosophy and then continue into the domain of the social sciences including psychology, political science, sociology, economics and management science. Next we look at trust in multidisciplinary research, ending with reputation research with an e-business focus. These divisions across domains are necessarily approximate because so much research crosses not just one, but several bordering domains.

Now, leaving reputation aside for a moment and starting with trust—what would the initial definition of trust be? According to the Cambridge English dictionary trust means "to believe that someone is good and honest and will not harm you, or that something is safe and reliable". So, trust is a belief that someone is good and honest and will not harm you, or that something is safe and reliable.

© The Author(s) 2018
D. Trček, *Trust and Reputation Management Systems*,
SpringerBriefs in Information Systems, DOI 10.1007/978-3-319-62374-0_2

2.1 Philosophy

It should come as no surprise that philosophers address trust rather extensively. In general, trust is of interest to philosophers mainly per se, and only secondarily utilitarian approach comes into focus. More precisely, philosophers usually pay attention to its cognitive dimension, or they pay attention to its normative dimension, which has two variants, the rational and non-rational [47].

Bearing in mind that *trust* in other domains, in particular in the computer science domain, is often used interchangeably with the term *belief* (as if these were synonyms) this is not the case in philosophy. Many philosophers are aware of this problem and clearly conceptualize the difference: "Several philosophers have observed that the relation between trust and evidence is different from that between belief and evidence. Indeed, some have suggested that there is a tension, or even incompatibility, between believing or acting on trust and believing or acting on evidence..." [31]. The same author states further "that reasons for trust are preemptive reasons for action or belief". He provides a supporting claim regarding the known resistance of trust to counter-evidence, suggesting that evidence and trust differ. What is probably most interesting is the conclusion that "trust is similar to an emotion: having an emotion involves being attuned to certain information, along with a tendency to ignore".

This last claim is worth emphasizing. It implies that trust is a matter of emotional factor(s). Some early researchers even claimed that trust is just another kind of emotion, as will be discussed later in this chapter. However, recent research in other areas suggests that trust is not related just to emotional processes in certain parts of the brain, but it also involves a rational component. Many philosophers explicitly acknowledge that trust has a rational component. Frost-Arnold claims that "trust is a rationally constrained cognitive attitude that can be adopted at will for the purpose of planning" [19]. Continuing with the rational dimension of trust, Tebben and Waterman developed an exchange-based account testimony where trust plays a key role. Epistemologically, a testimony is trustworthy when the agent behind it is competent and sincere [58].

In summary, the literature in the field of philosophy seriously considers both, the rational and non-rational dimensions of trust. Neither is excluded, although the precedence of one dimension over the other remains an open issue. This topic is a common thread that will be further addressed in the upcoming sections.

2.2 Trust Research in the Social Sciences Domain

Research on trust in the social sciences domain has a few decades longer tradition than in the computer and information sciences domain. The results of this research make valuable contributions to our understanding and provide important perspectives onto computational trust and reputation management. The emphasis in this section is placed on those works that help to shape such perspectives, enabling a better understanding of what trust is, its role, what its facets are, what are the driving factors behind trust, and its relationship to the decision making process.

Similarly to cases in other domains, many trust related research efforts in the social sciences domain are hard to place into one particular field. For example, research in sociology may have a strong economic focus, while psychology based research may aim at better management of organizations, and so on. Therefore, the below attribution of research works to particular fields was carried out first according to the field of origin of the research, and then according to the context of application.

2.2.1 *Psychology*

Generally speaking, and however surprising this may sounds, trust is still a rather infrequently addressed topic in psychology. Simpson nicely describes this as follows [55]: "Considering the centrality of trust in relationships across the lifespan, one might expect the topic would have received widespread theoretical and empirical attention; surprisingly, it has not."

Historically, one first attempt to address trust was made in the 1950s by Erikson in the area of developmental psychology. He defined eight stages of psychosocial development for a healthily developing human from infancy to adulthood, and the very first stage was about trust (and mistrust) development [18]. Erikson's emphasis on trust has been confirmed by many studies, such as by DeNeve and Cooper where it was found that trust is a good predictor of one's well-being [13].

But why is trust so important? According to [44], creating trust in someone or something has important consequences, which start with making one's life more predictable and creating a sense of community. Trust therefore makes it easier for people to work cooperatively, and cooperation can be an important advantage. It can make both parties better-off versus non-cooperative, purely selfish behaviour, which often will not (this subject was extensively studied by political sciences researcher Axelrod [2]).

Regarding the forms of trust that may be exhibited, the research in [55] differentiates trust into dispositional, i.e. general beliefs about the degree of trust in other people, and dyadic, i.e. interpersonal trust that is oriented toward a specific partner. In the latter case, four core principles take place. First, individuals gage the level of trust they can attribute to partners when it comes to strain-test situations, and when partners go against their own self-interest for the benefit of the relationship. Second, individuals may initiate trust testing situations to see if the attributed level of trust is warranted by a partner. Third, individual differences in orientation, self-esteem or self-differentiation affect the dynamics of trust in relationships, e.g. those with higher self-esteem and more differentiated self-concepts are more likely to experience trust. Fourth, in order to fully understand the dynamics and levels of trust, the dispositions and actions of both partners have to be taken into account. Considering now the model of dispositional trust, it is built around partners' dispositions that then influence each stage of trust evolution. This starts with the stage of entering trust situations, continuous with a transformation of motives and joint decisions, followed by the phase of attributions (and emotions and expectations), which is then followed by the perception of trust, and is finally followed by the perception of security.

Elaborating further the emergence of trust and trust driving factors, one rather expected result is that similar facial features (or facial resemblance) are a factor that increases trust [12]. But a more interesting result is that this resemblance can be generalized, such that in addition to knowledgeability, honesty and transparency, similarities in general are those that foster trust [17]. Some of the latest research has added new driving factors to this list, which are cues that may reveal how trustworthy a certain person is [60]. Specifically, the presence of certain non-verbal cues leads to more accurate predictions of other's behaviour in trust dependent scenarios. Another interesting recent study by Noah focused on the relationship between intelligence and general trust. This study is another example suggesting that generalized trust is correlated with intelligence [9].

If so, one old dilemma is one step closer to being resolved—trust cannot be just a matter of emotional processes that reside in sub-cortical areas of the brain, but it is also a matter of (neo)cortical activities, where "analytic intelligence" resides. This dilemma goes back to the interesting and pioneering research made by Plutchik [48]. He developed a psycho-evolutionary theory of emotion that included trust in the eight primary emotions: fear, anger, sadness, disgust, surprise, anticipation, joy plus trust. If this were the case, trust would be a matter of sub-cortical activities only. But taking into account what has been said so far (and will be further elaborated in the following sections), trust is likely related to both, (neo)cortical and sub-cortical brain processes, and therefore has both emotional, as well as rational dimensions.

2.2.2 Political Science

As in the field of psychology, trust remains a phenomenon that has yet to be more extensively researched in the domain of political science as well. Nevertheless, when it comes to trust, Axelrod is probably the most well known researcher [2]. Although Axelrod does not explicitly mention trust, his game theory based study of cooperation has a lot to do with it. One game of particular importance in Axelrod's research is the prisoner's dilemma. In this game (invented by Merrill Flood and Melvin Dresher at RAND Corporation in 1950s), you and your criminal mate have been captured and are held in separate cells. The evidence is rather weak, so the prosecutor, being a tough one, offers you the following: If you confess (defect) and your mate stays silent (cooperates) about the crime, you are free and the mate gets a 10 years sentence. If your mate confesses and you stay silent about the crime, you are sentenced to 10 years, while your mate goes free. If you both confess (defect), you both get 6 years each, while if you both remain silent (cooperate), you both go to prison for 6 months. The same offer is given to your mate, but you are not able to coordinate the plan with him.

The standard prisoner's dilemma has only one round, where defecting is the most rational strategy for both players. But Axelrod was interested in the evolutionary outcome of this game, so many rounds were considered. In this case, the optimal results turn out to be rather different from the single round. Axelrod used many strategies, but the most beneficial one was the tit-for-tat strategy that goes as follows. One should cooperate on the first move, and subsequently reciprocate what the other player does on the previous move. Put another way, the best performance strategy is to be nice, but once defection takes place, retaliate immediately.[1]

More recent, explicitly trust focused research can be found in [7] where trust in government and fiscal adjustments is studied. Authors suggest that trust and credibility play an important role in both, monetary and fiscal policies. Now the problem is how to measure trust in institutions as specifically as possible, and not just using an overshot approach by asking about general trust. One answer can be found in [40], where the authors present a general framework for measuring trust in public institutions. This framework results in an index of trust that has been tested in various countries. The obtained results confirm the rather common view that such trust is highest among Scandinavian countries, while being significantly lower in former communist countries, Iberian, and Mediterranean countries.

To conclude this section, it is worth adding that political scientists expose the possibility of subtle and unintended slips when dealing with trust. The research by Scnheider warns that real understanding of what political trust truly means in various cultural and regime settings may be an elusive endeavour. Typical survey questions cannot pinpoint the nature and content of the studied beliefs, nor the precise reasons for mistrust, either [53].

2.2.3 Sociology

Research in the domain of sociology generally indicates that trust has many positive influences on societies. It can be seen as a kind of social capital that makes coordination and cooperation within societies possible. Consequently, trust correlates positively with productivity, health and lower crime rates in society overall. However, many situations in societies are characterized by complexity and uncertainty. This uncertainty is largely due to other individuals in a society, so the need for trust stems from the lack of detailed knowledge about other's abilities and motivations to act as promised [14]. Pushing this line of reasoning to the extreme, it can be stated that trust would not be an issue if one could accurately

---

[1]This game is a typical zero-sum game, which means that the rewards are fixed so the more is assigned to one player, the less remains there for the other player. However, life is not always a zero-sum game.

assess the reasoning or functioning of another individual that one is depending upon [23]. What trust enables is better coping with such uncertain situations by decreasing complexity through reduction of options that have to be considered in given situations [38].

But how do sociologists address and understand the process of trust formation? There exist two basic approaches. According to the first one, trust can be linked to a rational evaluation of the reliability of people through concrete experience or information, while according to the second one trust is based on the moral predispositions of individuals [59]. However, social scientists acknowledge that it is likely that combinations of both also take place, as emphasized in [64].

How do sociologists address different facets of trust? Some initial foundations were set in the mid-90s by McAllister [42] and elaborated on in more detail later by others like Chowdhury [10]. In principle, sociologists recognize two forms of trust, the first one being cognition-based and the second one being affect-based. In the first case trust is based on an individual's thinking about confidence in the other entity, i.e. it is based on good reasons that justify trustworthiness. In the second case trust is based on emotional bonds between individuals that involve mutual care and concern.

One interesting kind of research, rather specific to sociology, is about the erosion of trust in relation to legal norms in business, as well as in private settings [49]. In business settings, the consequences include weakening of modesty, honour, responsibility, and attitudes of hard work, while in private settings this means the erosion of traditional family values, increased divorces, and the disappearance of intergenerational cohesion. This work also identifies trust driving factors as generally perceived by sociology community. It starts with macro-social factors (like income inequality, hierarchical vs. non-hierarchical religions, ethnic diversity), and continues with state driven political-institutional factors (like support for cooperation, prevention of corruption or fraud, inequality reduction). They further include individual demographic characteristics (like gender, age, educational level), and end with personality traits (like optimism), and participation in social activities (like membership of voluntary organisations). This work also implies that social and moral norms may play a crucial role in generalized, i.e. social trust, which is a key pillar of social capital.

An apparatus that is used to measure generalized, interpersonal trust in countries around the world is World Values Survey (WVS). The key question is the following: "Generally speaking, would you say that most people can be trusted or that you need to be very careful in dealing with people?" Now, how WVS is understood is another important issue that is addressed in [11], where authors actually tackle the epistemological validity of this apparatus by providing results of an experimental study in Brazil. While aiming to address the understanding of trust among Brazilians with higher education, they found that the WVS partially hits the mark, and partially misses it. Actually, Brazilians, when asked this question, often implicitly think of friends and relatives, so their responses are not necessarily about general interpersonal trust. To further complicate matters when it comes to the measuring the trust, Beugelsdijk suggests that the WVS likely measures trust in institutions

[4]. This dichotomy can be partially understood by cultural backgrounds where these studies have been conducted. To further address this problem, Inglehart and Welzel used Freedom House scores as democracy indicators, and corruption scores by the World Bank. They found out that there is notable positive correlation between interpersonal trust and democracy (including low-corruption level) [28].

2.2.4   Economics

An increasing number of studies provides supporting evidence for the belief that generalized trust (i.e. trust in strangers) results in benefits to the economy, while lack of this kind of trust negatively affects economic growth [62]. One reason is that trust plays the role of a lubricant in economic exchange [1]. Furthermore, when exchange of goods and services is the focus, trust in cooperative behaviour by trading partners can lead to lower transaction costs [62]. Therefore it is reasonable to conclude that when an economy consists of enterprises that run with low transaction costs, this gives the whole economy a competitive advantage. So trust pays off.

Probably the most distinguishing contribution in economics related to trust research is the measuring of trust in the sub-field of experimental economics. This measuring is most often carried out using the Trust game, which was designed by Berg at al. in 1995 [3]. In this game (also referred to as the Investment game) player A goes first. She decides on an amount of money X to be given to player B. This amount can be from 0 EUR to 100 EUR. If some amount is sent, B receives three-times the given amount, i.e. $3X$. Now it is B's turn to send back Y from the interval $[0, 3X]$. The pay-off for player A is therefore $100 - X + Y$, while for player B it is $3X - Y$. Trust is considered as follows: when A sends money, she takes a risk on B and must trust him to reciprocate by sending back at least X in compensation. Consequently, B is trustworthy if he sends back $Y \geq X$ (and not trustworthy otherwise).

The results of this game show that people generally behave in a trusting way. But one should be aware of the game's limitations. It is rather sensible to assume that the amount of money involved changes the attitudes towards gains and losses. This is also confirmed in studies like [33], where authors state that "... when dealing with smaller amounts of capital, people prefer to take more risk, compared to larger amounts" (they attribute this situation to *loss aversion* as discovered by Kahneman and Tversky [29]).

There are interesting variants of the Trust game like the one where people play it with other people's money [36]. This study shows that when playing on behalf of others the first players (the senders) do not behave significantly different in cases when they manage their own money. However, second-players (the receivers) return significantly less money in such cases. Further, and interestingly, women return significantly less money in such role than men.

The Trust game is not the only game that experimental economics uses. Another often deployed game is the Dictator game [8]. In this game the first player decides for a split of an endowment, while the second player receives the remainder, allocated by the first player. Many studies show that first players frequently allocate money to receivers despite the reduced amount of money that they would receive otherwise. It should be added that this game is considered as a kind of degenerative game because receivers are passive collaborators without an ability to strategically influence the outcome.

The above mentioned games are not the only ones used in experimental economics. Other examples include the Sender-receiver game [24] and Investment game [32]. But whatever the experimental economic game, the question is whether (and to what extent) cooperation between players in such games can serve as evidence of trust (or reputation for that matter) [20]. Experimental economists presume that an entity should exhibit a level of trust in transactions that is equal to the trustworthiness of the other party. If this requirement is met, efficient markets are enabled [6]. Another open question remains how to quantify trust levels. One suggestion is to look at the correlation between profit margin and transaction cost [50].

Experimental economics is not the only sub-branch of economics that is researching trust. Analyses of questionnaires and statistical data provide another venue, as shown in [26], where authors check whether trust is affected by inequality in market vs. non-market conditions. Inequality seems to have a strong negative impact on trust, especially when inequalities are known. It is interesting that people seem to be prepared to live more easily with inequalities under market conditions than in non-market settings. This is likely due to the commonly accepted social agreement in liberal democracies that the market is the foundation of economics. If so, does competition inadvertently have to result in inequalities?

Let's conclude this section with political economics where Fukuyama is probably the most visible author to be addressing trust [21]. Based on his study of various cultures through the prism of trust he claims that their economical prosperity and well being is crucially dependent on trust. Now how trust is actually achieved is the key question, and to obtain an answer Fukuyama studies extreme cases like the United States on one hand (as an example of a highly individualized society) and Italy on the other (as an example where family businesses play a central role). In the former case Fukuyama claims that trust is rooted in the affirmative belief in institutions (like judicial system), while in the latter case trust is rooted in tight familial networks.

2.2.5 Management Science

When it comes to the effects of trust on organisations, there are two focuses—one is an intra-organisational one, and the other is an inter-organisational one. Starting with the latter, a few decades ago it was shown that trust is vital for successful inter-organizational cooperation and the effectiveness of organisations overall [42]. Trust may also reduce organizational complexity [22]. Furthermore, in those businesses where trust is lacking, information exchange is hampered, risk of misunderstandings increases, and poor-decision making becomes a serious issue [25, 27]. Similar effects apply to trust in inter-organisational settings, where some concrete effects include successful long-term relationships [34], while inter-firm transaction costs are reduced [5].

However, intra-organisational trust is certainly the first step. In order to form interpersonal trust relationships within an organization, appropriate conditions have to be fulfilled [56]. First, opportunistic behaviour has to be prevented. Second, positive relational signals exchange has to be stimulated while negative ones have to be avoided. Third, trust enhancing organizational policies have to be put into place. But these general rules should be further elaborated to uncover the many hidden trust formation factors and their dynamics within organizations. So, for example, organizational trust can result from factors like the owner's personality in small organizations, while in large organizations it is the result of a well defined decision structure, supported by the organizational culture, which creates predictable (aka trustworthy) behaviour [65].

Similar to psychologists, researchers in this area state that establishing trust is an interactive process that is based on positive feedback that reinforces initial trustworthy behaviour, so that trust gradually increases [63]. This evolution is elaborated more deeply in [37], where it is shown that trust evolves in three stages. The first one is the so called calculus based stage where one key factor is the fear of punishment, while another key factor is anticipation of reward. In the second stage, we see a transition to knowledge based trust, which is based on information from long term experience that enables predictability of another's behaviour. The last stage is so called identification based trust, where parties know each other so well that they can anticipate the behaviour of one another. Taking another perspective on the above three-stages process, Mayer-Davis and Schoormann emphasize two key dimensions of trust: one is its benevolence component, which has a large affective content, and the other is its competence component, which places emphasis on the cognitive content [41].

One specific issue in this domain is managing virtual teams. This is a special challenge that has emerged recently and is particularly characteristic of the software industry. In this case trust is assumed to be an indispensable asset, but how can inter-personal trust grow in environments where all the other usual signals are missing? An intuitive judgement would be that informal, non-work-related conversations like cheap talk are facilitating it. Wang and Redmiles adapted the concept of cheap talk as understood in the economic literature and deployed evolutionary game theory to virtual teams to obtain insights into interpersonal cooperation dynamics. Using this apparatus they confirmed quantitatively and qualitatively that cheap talk over the Internet did facilitate the emergence of trust, and consequently, the probability of cooperation [61]. However, research presented in [39] somewhat opposes the generally accepted view that trust in virtual teams leads to positive outcomes. The authors provide evidence that in virtual teams those with distrust significantly outperformed control groups in the context of a non-routine decision-making tasks.

A good conclusion of this brief overview is that trust plays an important role in management science. It can be treated as a major environmental factor that may affect organizations in terms of stability and density [43], which is important because stable, prosperous organisations are a basis for stable and prosperous societies.

2.3 Multidisciplinary Research

Multidisciplinary research focused on trust is particularly rich in the areas of human computer interactions and e-commerce. One probably main reason for this is that computer and information technology mediated communications differ significantly from face to face interactions. So, on the one hand, our lives are increasingly dependent on e-media, where ordinary signals are absent, or are at least distorted (social theory refers to this situation as channel reduction [15]), while on the other hand evolutionary acquired trust cues can provide little support. Consequently, this reduction in information leads to increased uncertainty [54].

Clearly, in the case of e-media some initial trust trigger needs to exist to enable engagement in interactions that may leave both parties better off than if no interaction would have taken place. A key question is how to foster interaction in e-environments through supporting trustworthy behaviour? One framework that provides some answers has been defined by Riegelsbereger. It takes into account the relevant research in psychology, sociology and economics, and identifies two kinds of factors: contextual properties and the actor's intrinsic properties [51]. While contextual properties include those elements that are motivation based (be it because of temporal, social, or institutional embeddedness), the actor's intrinsic properties include ability, motivation based on internalized norms, and benevolence. So, contextual properties can motivate rational self-interested trustees to meet expectations, but fail to explain how actors behave internally. And that is where the extension with intrinsic properties comes in, such is when a trustee does not look for monetary gains, but for gratification, which is in line with his or her moral or ethical beliefs.

Another branch of research, focused on fostering trust in e-media environments, is described in [52]. The process of interpersonal trust formation is given as a basis, which consists of inputs (signals and signs), cognitive processes (collection and selection of information, assessment of trustworthiness, assessment of the situation, trust state, trust decision, context), and outputs (trusting behaviour, interaction and evaluation). Bound to this model is the so called trustworthiness antecedent schema (TWAN) that consists of the following categories:

- communality, i.e. personal characteristics that the trustor and the trustee have in common;
- ability, i.e. knowledge, competence, skills;

- benevolence, i.e. willingness to help, sharing faith in intentions, receptivity, friendliness, kindness, commitment;
- internalized norms, i.e. integrity, fairness, loyalty, discretion, honesty;
- accountability, i.e. reliability, consistency, persistence and responsibility.

TWAN sounds appealing and convincing, its claims are based on an extensive literature review, but experimental verification, to the best of our knowledge, is yet to be carried out.

And what can be said about trust in information systems and technologies as such? A piece of research in [57] provides answers by focusing on a so called network of trust, where the following entities are involved: information systems, users, providers, community of internet users, and the internet itself. The main finding is that users' trust in the information system (IS) is a major driver of this very IS to be used by the users. Of comparable importance to trust in the IS is trust in the provider of IT services. So one kind of trust is about trust in technological artefacts as such, while the other kind of trust is about trusting humans that manage these artefacts. A similar study about trust with relation to technological artefacts as such is discussed in [30]. By using surveys for structural equation modelling it is experimentally shown that to increase this kind of trust, organisations should seriously consider their platforms certifications. Similarly, an analysis in [35] shows that visual, reputational, and contextual factors (starting with graphic design and going as far as public relations) are important to generate trust in on-line services (or information systems in general).

This multidisciplinary-overview will be rounded up by focusing on the cross-roads of the fields of sociology, technology and law. In [45] the authors analyse social orderings that rely upon individuals' ability to make extended commitments to one another. To support such commitments, an efficient legal system is needed. But at least as crucial for social orders is an understanding of these commitments by individuals. So authors base commitments categorisation on the legal perspective and extend this into a commitment hierarchy "that reflects the social, legal, and technological context in which it arises". Authors warn that changes to any of these factors modify commitment choices and the social ordering that emerges. Consequently, such changes may lead to significant social dislocation. And where is trust in this context? It is in the commitment hierarchy that starts with trust, continues with reputation, goes on with contracts, fiduciary duty and ends with regulation.

2.4 Linking Trust to Reputation

This chapter will conclude with coverage of reputation, because only trust has been the focus so far. The reason for this is the following. It is sensible to say that trust is a phenomenon of a higher precedence, which is in principle a precursor to reputation. Trust can exist in the case of a single individual, while reputation makes sense in the case of existence of some community. Thus reputation can be considered as a kind of reflection of trust spread over a community—it may be trust from many members that results in one entity's reputation, but once this entity's reputation is in place, this reputation may be a generator of trust. Another argument as to why trust should come first and reputation second, is data about how often one or the other term is looked for in search engines or mentioned in research papers. In case of trust vs. reputation the typical ratio is approximately three to one in favour of trust.[2]

The next thing that needs addressing is the definition of reputation, where one again enters the territory of rather elusive phenomenon. The Cambridge dictionary defines reputation as "the opinion that people in general have about someone or something, or how much respect or admiration someone or something receives, based on past behaviour or character". Similarly, the Merriam-Webster dictionary defines reputation as "the common opinion that people have about someone or something, or the way in which people think of someone or something".

These two definitions provide a sufficient basis for our purposes. Although they do not mention trust, trust and reputation are, as we know, in close relationship and some research that address this relationship follow.

To illustrate this relationship in e-environments the research in [16] links the two phenomena as follows. Trust is considered as a mechanism for reducing perceived risk that comprises three dimensions. The first one is the person's trusting attitudes toward the vendor, the second is the person's trusting attitudes towards the system and the self, and the third is the person's trusting intention to buy from a vendor on the Internet. This empirical study shows that a person's trusting intention is mostly influenced by her attitude toward the vendor and if the person's experience with a particular vendor is low, then reputation comes in by enhancing (or reducing) trust.

To illustrate the relationship between trust and reputation in a wider context, there is an interesting analysis in [46]. Both phenomena are considered as a kind of commitment mechanisms that underpin social orderings. By further narrowing this to business commitments the authors provide a hierarchy, where trust is positioned as the first mechanism, reputation as the second, then come contracts, and finally regulation. Interestingly, they also note that "reputational enforcement is frequently conflated with trust-based commitments".

*   *   *

The goal of this chapter is to provide readers with sufficient—but not overly detailed—insights into trust and reputation phenomena. By doing so the chapter paves the way for the core topics that come next. These are the models and solutions for computational trust and reputation management.

---

[2]On the 10th of August, 2016, Google search returned almost one billion hits for trust, while reputation hits amounted to some 300 millions. Similarly, on SpringerLink there was 400,000+ hits for trust, and a bit more than 170,000 for reputation, while ACM Digital Library returned almost 5000 hits for trust, and some 1000 hits for reputation.

References

1. K.J. Arrow. *The Limits of Organization*. Fels Center of Government Series (Norton, New York, 1974)
2. R.M. Axelrod, *The Evolution of Cooperation* (Basic Books, New York, 1984)
3. J. Berg, J. Dickaut, K. McCabe, Trust, reciprocity and social history. Games Econ. Behav. **95**(10), 122–142 (1995)
4. S. Beugelsdijk, A note on the theory and measurement of trust in explaining differences in economic growth. Camb. J. Econ. **30**(3), 371–387 (2006)
5. N. Bharadwaj, K. Matsuno, Investigating the antecedents and outcomes of customer firm transaction cost savings in a supply chain relationship. J. Bus. Res. **59**(1), 62–72 (2006)
6. S. Braynov, T. Sandholm, Contracting with uncertain level of trust. Comput. Intell. **18**(4), 501–514, 11 (2002)
7. D. Bursian, A.J. Weichenrieder, J. Zimmer, Trust in government and fiscal adjustments. Int. Tax Public Financ. **22**(4), 663–682 (2015)
8. C. Camerer, *Behavioral Game Theory: Experiments in Strategic Interaction* (Princeton University Press, Princeton, 2003)
9. N. Carl, C.F. Billari, Generalized trust and intelligence in the united states. PloS one **9**(3), 1–10 (2014)
10. S. Chowdhury, The role of affect- and cognition-based trust in complex knowledge sharing. J. Manag. Issues **17**(3), 310–326 (2005)
11. J.A. de Aquino, The meaning of trust for Brazilians with higher education. Soc. Indic. Res. **130**, 1–25 (2015)
12. L.M. DeBruine, Facial resemblance enhances trust. Proc. R. Soc. Lond. B Biol. Sci. **269**(1498), 1307–1312 (2002)
13. M.K. DeNeve, H. Cooper, The happy personality: a-meta analysis of 137 personality traits and subjective well-being. Psychol. Bull. **98**(124), 197–229 (1998)
14. M. Deutsch, Trust and suspicion. J. Confl. Resolut. **2**(4), 265–279 (1958)
15. N. Döring, *Sozialpsychologie des Internet. Die Bedeutung des Internet für Kommunikationsprozesse, Identitäten, soziale Beziehungen und Gruppen*. Hogrefe-Verlag, 2, vollst. ünerarb. u. erw. a. edn. (2003)
16. S. Einwiller, When reputation engenders trust: an empirical investigation in business-to-consumer electronic commerce. Electron. Mark. **13**(3), 196–209 (2003)
17. J.R. Eiser, M.P White, A psychological approach to understanding how trust is built and lost in the context of risk. Presentation at the Social Contexts and Responses to Risk conference, Taking Stock of Trust, December (2005)
18. E. Erikson, *Childhood and Society* (W.W. Norton & Co, New York, 1950)
19. K. Frost-Arnold, The cognitive attitude of rational trust. Synthese **191**(9), 1957–1974 (2014)
20. D. Fudenberg, J. Tirole, *Game Theory* (MIT Press, Cambridge, 1991)
21. F. Fukuyama, *Trust - The Social Virtues and the Creation of Prosperity* (Free Press, New York, 1995)
22. D. Gefen, E-commerce: the role of familiarity and trust. Omega **28**(6), 725–737 (2000)
23. A. Giddens, *The Consequences of Modernity* (Stanford University Press, Stanford, 2016/05/13 1990)
24. M.Y. Gurdal, A. Ozdogan, I. Saglam, Truth-telling and trust in sender–receiver games with intervention: an experimental study. Rev. Econ. Des. **18**(2), 83–103 (2014)
25. P. Häkkinen, What makes learning and understanding in virtual teams so difficult? CyberPsychol. Behav. **7**(2), 201–206 (2004)
26. H. Hargreaves, P. Shaun, J.H.W. Tan, D.J. Zizzo, Trust, inequality and the market. Theor. Decis. **74**(3), 311–333 (2013)
27. F. Hartman, The role of trust in project management, in *Managing Business by Projects*, ed. by K.A. Artto, K. Kahkönen, K. Koskinen, vol. 1, Espoo (Project Management Association Finland and Nordnet, Elsinki, 1999)

28. R. Inglehart, C. Welzel, *Modernization, Cultural Change, and Democracy: The Human Development Sequence* (Cambridge University Press, New York, NY, 2005)
29. D. Kahneman, A. Tversky, Choices, values, and frames. Am. Psychol. **39**(4), 341–350 (1984)
30. D. Ke, A. Chen, C. Su, Online trust-building mechanisms for existing brands: the moderating role of the e-business platform certification system. Electron. Commer. Res. **16**(2), 189–216 (2016)
31. A. Keren, Trust and belief: a preemptive reasons account. Synthese **191**(12), 2593–2615 (2014)
32. C. Keser, Experimental games for the design of reputation management systems. IBM Syst. J. **42**(3), 498–506 (2003)
33. G. Klein, Z. Shtudiner, Trust in others: does it affect investment decisions? Qual. Quant. **49** 1–19 (2015)
34. D. Koehn. Should we trust in trust? Am. Bus. Law J. **34**(2), 183–204 (1996)
35. I.P. Kuzheleva-Sagan, N.A. Suchkova, Designing trust in the internet services. AI Soc. **31**(3), 381–392 (2016)
36. O. Kvaløy, M. Luzuriaga, Playing the trust game with other people's money. Exp. Econ. **17**(4), 615–630 (2014)
37. R.J. Lewicki, B.B. Bunker, Developing and maintaining trust in work relationships (1996)
38. J.D. Lewis, A. Weigert, Trust as a social reality. Soc. Forces **63**(4), 967–985 (1985)
39. P.B. Lowry, R.M. Schuetzler, J.S. Giboney, T.A. Gregory, Is trust always better than distrust? the potential value of distrust in newer virtual teams engaged in short-term decision-making. Group Decis. Negot. **24**(4), 723–752 (2015)
40. M. Marozzi, Measuring trust in European public institutions. Soc. Indic. Res. **123**(3), 879–895 (2015)
41. R.C. Mayer, J.H. Davis, F.D. Schoorman, An integrative model of organizational trust. Acad. Manag. Rev. **20**(3), 709–734 (1995)
42. D.J. McAllister, Affect and cognition-based trust as foundations for interpersonal cooperation in organizations. Acad. Manag. Rev. **38**(1), 24–59 (1995)
43. B. Mcevily, V. Perrone, A. Zaheer, Trust as an organizing principle. Organ. Sci. **14**(1), 91–103 (2003)
44. A.B. Misztal, *Trust in Modern Societies* (Polity/Wiley, New York, 1996)
45. A.D. Morrison, W.J. Wilhelm, Trust, reputation and law: the evolution of commitment in investment banking (2013)
46. A.D. Morrison, W.J. Wilhelm, Trust, reputation, and law: the evolution of commitment in investment banking. J. Legal Anal. **7**(2), 363–420 (2015)
47. N. Pedersen, L.L. Jang, K. Ahlström-Vij, K. Kappel, Rational trust. Synthese **191**(9), 1953–1955 (2014)
48. R. Plutchik, The nature of emotions: clinical implications, in *Emotions and Psychopathology*, ed. by M. Clynes, J. Panksepp (Springer US, Boston, MA, 1988), pp. 1–20
49. M. Popper, Social trust, norms and morality. Hum. Aff. **23**(3), 443–457 (2013)
50. P. Resnick, R. Zeckhauser, J. Swanson, K. Lockwood, The value of reputation on eBay: a controlled experiment. Exp. Econ. **9**(2), 79–101 (2006)
51. J. Riegelsberger, M.A. Sasse, J.D. McCarthy, The mechanics of trust: a framework for research and design. Int. J. Hum. Comput. Stud. **62**(3), 381–422 (2005)
52. E. Rusman, J. Van Bruggen, P. Sloep, R. Koper, Fostering trust in virtual project teams: towards a design framework grounded in a trustworthiness antecedents (TWAN) schema. Int. J. Hum. Comput. Stud. **68**(11), 834–850 (2010)
53. I. Schneider, Can we trust measures of political trust? assessing measurement equivalence in diverse regime types. Soc. Indic. Res. 1–22 (2016). doi:10.1007/s11205-016-1400-8
54. B. Shneiderman, Designing trust into online experiences. Commun. ACM **43**(12), 57–59 (2000)
55. J.A. Simpson, Psychological foundations of trust. Curr. Dir. Psychol. Sci. **16**(5), 264–268 (2007)
56. F.E. Six, Building interpersonal trust within organizations: a relational signalling perspective. J. Manag. Gov. **11**(3), 285–309 (2007)

57. M. Söllner, A. Hoffmann, M.J. Leimeister, Why different trust relationships matter for information systems users. Eur. J. Inf. Syst. **25**(3), 274–287 (2016)
58. N. Tebben, P.J. Waterman, Counterfeit testimony: lies, trust, and the exchange of information. Philos. Stud. **173**, 1–17 (2016)
59. L. Torpe, H. Lolle, Identifying social trust in cross-country analysis: do we really measure the same? Soc. Indic. Res. **103**(3), 481–500 (2011)
60. P. Valdesolo, Psychologists uncover hidden signals of trust - using a robot. Sci. Am. **307**, 201–213, 1 (2013)
61. Y. Wang, D. Redmiles, Cheap talk, cooperation, and trust in global software engineering. Empir. Softw. Eng. 1–35 (2015). doi:10.1007/s10664-015-9407-3
62. P.J. Zak, S. Knack, Trust and growth. Econ. J. **111**(470), 295–321 (2001)
63. D.E. Zand, Trust and managerial problem solving. Adm. Sci. Q. **17**(2), 229–239 (1972)
64. L. Zanin, R. Radice, G. Marra, Estimating the effect of perceived risk of crime on social trust in the presence of endogeneity bias. Soc. Indic. Res. **114**(2), 523–547 (2013)
65. L.G. Zucker, Production of trust: institutional sources of economic structure, 1840–1920. Res. Organ. Behav. **8**, 53–111 (1986)

Chapter 3
Computational Trust and Reputation Management

Trust, but verify.
(Russian proverb)

Computational trust and reputation management now has a 20 years long tradition. As these services are tightly coupled to e-environments, the need for them has coincided with the proliferation of the e-business paradigm beginning in the 1990s. Consequently, the greater the proliferation of e-environments, the greater the need for such services. If trust and reputation play such an important role in different areas of our lives, e-environments can be no exception.

The evolution of trust and reputation management in these environments can be roughly divided into three epochs that are marked by three surveys in this field. The first one was written in 2000 by Grandison and Sloman [15] and covers the era when trust was mainly used in relation to traditional hard security provisioning systems. The second epoch can be marked by a survey written in 2007 by Josang et al. [19]. This one already covered trust and reputation systems that focused on trust and reputation at their core. The third epoch is marked by the survey written in 2013 by Pinyol and Sabater-Mir [30], when the field started to emerge as a kind of infrastructural area for other application areas.

Before going into the details of computational trust and reputation management systems, the thus far given definitions will have to be reconsidered. These definitions were actually addressing trust among individuals, among social structures, or among individuals and social structures. However, defining trust and reputation for technological artefacts, particularly those based on information technology, is very important as well.

Thus we will start this chapter with the definition proposed by Prof. Dr. D.J. Denning, which says that "trust is an assessment that is driven by experience, shared through a network of people interactions and continually remade each time the system is used" [12]. This definition provides an appropriate basis that we will extend to cover the scope of our domain of interest—e-business: *Trust is an assessment, based on a belief that someone is good and honest, or that something is*

© The Author(s) 2018
D. Trček, *Trust and Reputation Management Systems*,
SpringerBriefs in Information Systems, DOI 10.1007/978-3-319-62374-0_3

safe and reliable. This belief is driven by experiences and is dynamically adjusted through direct or indirect feed-back information provided by a given environment.

Such a belief can come in various forms and should not be interpreted narrowly. Very often (probably due to historical reasons) this belief is stated in terms of probabilities, e.g. Gambetta treated trust as "the subjective probability by which an individual expects that another individual performs a given action on which its welfare depends" [13] (this kind of trust is also referred to as reliability trust). Yet for other authors the above mentioned assessment is embodied in "the extent to which one party is willing to depend on something or somebody in a given situation with a feeling of relative security, even though negative consequences are possible" [22].

Having trust specified precisely, what would the definition of trust management be? Trust management will be defined by adapting the definition given in [9], which is focused on artificial intelligent agent environments. Modifying it to cover e-business purposes the definition is as follows: *Trust management stands for procedures that are based on symbol-based modelling and calculi, which cover a human or artificial agent's inner trust processes related to other agents, services or technological artefacts.* And finally, a trust management system can be defined as follows: *A trust management system is on information technology based system aimed at supporting or automating trust management procedures.*

Throughout this chapter we will also be dealing with taxonomies, categorisations and classifications, therefore these terms have to be clarified to ensure their common understanding. According to the Cambridge English dictionary, *a taxonomy is a system for naming and organizing things (especially plants and animals) into groups that share similar qualities* [5]. Furthermore, the term *classification means the act or process of dividing things into groups according to their type*, while *categorization means the act of putting people or things into groups with the same features*. As it follows, classification and categorisation can be used rather interchangeably, while taxonomy follows as a result of one of these processes.

Last but not least, the terms *models* and *methods* will be used extensively. According to Cambridge English dictionary—and with some reinterpretation—*a model is a representation of something in words, numbers, or other symbols for that matter, while methods are particular operations implied by the model for its implementation*. Consider this example: A set of differential equations may characterize a model of a particular economic theory, where the model is subject to some mathematical operations, which represent methods in a broader sense. Being aware of this semantic difference between the two terms we will use them in this book rather interchangeably when it comes to trust and reputation.

3.1 Computational Trust Models and Methods

Conceptual models provide many benefits that range from deeper understanding of the phenomenon at hand to its practical realisation or treatment. Many examples can be found in various scientific domains that support such claim, e.g.:

- In physics, the core model is the Standard Model that explains how the basic blocks that matter is composed of interact one with another, and how they are governed during these interactions by the four fundamental forces: the strong force, the weak force, the electromagnetic force, and the gravitational force [8].
- In computer communications, there are several complex tasks, divided into functional layers that form layered stacks, comprising so called reference models such as TCP/IP [10]. In these models, the functions of each layer are specified, the interaction points between layers are defined together with the format and semantics of the exchanged data, and the protocols are introduced to enable one layer to meaningfully communicate with another layer.
- In neuroscience, brain networks are modelled as large classes of information processing systems that share important organizational principles in common, including the property of a hierarchical modularity and modularity on several topological scales [24].

In this respect, the computational trust (and reputation) management domain is no exception. However, it lacks a conceptual (or reference) model for trust, its related factors and their dynamic interplay during the trust formation process. The previous analysis of trust through various perspectives enables us to introduce the conceptual model that is given in Fig. 3.1, which extends the one presented in [40].

In Fig. 3.1 α denotes an agent's (trust) assessment value, and A stands for the set of all agents' possible assessments, so that $\alpha \in A$. This assessment has two forms—the first one is the inner one, called major assessment $\bar{\alpha}$, which is the intimate trust. The second one is the minor assessment, $\underline{\alpha}$, which is communicated, but may differ from the major one due to weak communication skills or manipulations. Trust assessment then enters the decision-making process that is modelled by two mappings, one defining a concrete action or deed, η, the other, ς, driving the uttered, communicated assessment. The concrete action of the agent based on its assessments belongs to the set of all actions, while the concrete communicated assessment becomes a member of all the communicated assessments. These two sets, Δ and A, together with time values (elements of the set T) that are needed to cover temporal dynamics, represent inputs to function φ. Function φ takes the whole context into account, the communicated assessments and deeds by other agents in a community, weights them accordingly using function Ξ, and derives new values for major and minor assessments.

Given an agent $agent_i$, its conceptual model is intended to capture trust assessments to be used at time $t + 1$, assuming we know trust assessments at time t. Therefore the actual calculation of new trust assessments for agent $agent_i$ are given

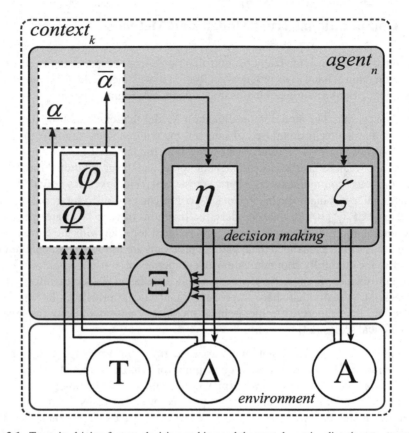

Fig. 3.1 Trust, its driving factors, decision making and the trust dynamics dictating structure

as follows:

$$\bar{\alpha}_i(t+1) = \bar{\varphi}_i(A(t), \Delta(t), \Xi_i(t)),$$
$$\underline{\alpha}_i(t+1) = \underline{\varphi}_i(A(t), \Delta(t), \Xi_i(t)). \tag{3.1}$$

Once the conceptual model has been characterized, the next step is to provide a suitable taxonomy, as there exists no widely accepted taxonomy of trust management systems (the same applies for reputation management systems). Before providing it, we will give a historical overview of trust management systems. Based on this evolutionary overview, a taxonomy appropriate for the purposes of this book will follow (trust management will be covered first, followed by reputation management).

3.1.1 Marsh's Formalism

The first attempt to extensively address computational trust was carried out in 1994 by Stephen P. Marsh [21]. He introduced a formalism to characterize and deal with trust in a precise way, and which is implementable in computing environments. In this formalism (which is largely based on trust research in the social sciences and has emphasis on artificial agents) the basic elements are agents, sets of agents, agents' societies, situations, knowledge, importance, utility, basic trust, general trust, situational trust, and time. These elements' naming, representations and ranges are given in Table 3.1.

The expression $T_x(y)^t$ plays the central role, stating how much agent x trusted agent y at time t. Similarly, $T_x(y, \alpha)^t$ states how much x trusted y at time t in situation α. Furthermore, the notation $U_x(\alpha)$ states the utility x gains from situation α. Additionally, the importance of a situation for an agent is denoted by $I_x(\alpha)$, while $K_x(y)$ states the knowledge of x about agent y. Clearly, the smaller the trust, utility, etc., the more negative its value (and vice versa).

Knowledge refers to any fact (denoted using propositional logic) indicating that agent x knows agent y, while general trust refers to the amount of trust that agent x has in agent y (when narrowed to a particular situation this general trust distils into a situational trust). As to utility, this should be considered in the traditional economic sense of the word. It is supposed to state a more objective treatment of a situation, while the importance refers to the same situation, but from an agent's point of view (which, being subjective, may differ from the objective utility). And what is then basic trust? This is trust that is the result of all past experiences of an agent in all situations, and is actually not related to any other particular situation or agent per se.

Finally, individual agents are members of the universal set of all agents, and particular subsets of agents are therefore $\mathcal{A}, \mathcal{B}, \ldots$. Given these sets of agents, distinguishing subsets can be identified, called societies and denoted as $S_1, S_2, \ldots$. A society is defined by one or more common characteristics that apply to all of its members, such as belonging to certain community (e.g. if set A denotes certain

Table 3.1 The elements of the Marsh trust formalism

Description	Representation	Range
Agents	$a, b, \ldots$	$a, \ldots, z$
Sets of agents	$\mathcal{A}, \mathcal{B}, \ldots$	$\mathcal{A}, \ldots, \mathcal{Z}$
Agents' societies	$S_1, S_2, \ldots$	$S_1, \ldots, S_n$
Situations	$\alpha, \beta, \ldots$	$\alpha, \ldots, \omega$
Knowledge	$K_x(y)^t$	True/false
Importance	$I_x(\alpha)^t$	$[0, 1]$
Utility	$U_x(\alpha)^t$	$[-1, +1]$
Basic trust	T_x^t	$[-1, +1)$
General trust	T_x^t	$[-1, +1)$
Situational trust	$T_x(y, \alpha)^t$	$[-1, +1)$

state citizens, societies $S_1, S_2, \ldots$ may denote certain city communities, then the corresponding county community, and so on).

Based on these descriptive definitions it is possible to model trust as follows:

$$T_x(y, \alpha)^t = U_x(\alpha)^t \cdot I_x(\alpha)^t \cdot \widehat{T_x(y)}^t \qquad (3.2)$$

This equation states the estimated situational trust of agent x in agent y given as the weighted probability (the weights being U and I) acting on the estimated general trust $\widehat{T_x(y)}^t$ in a certain situation α at a certain time t. More precisely, $U_x(\alpha)^t$ represents the utility that x may gain from a situation α, while $I_x(\alpha)^t$ represents the importance of the situation α for agent x. The estimate of general trust $\widehat{T_x(y)}^t$ takes into account all relevant data with respect to $T_x(y)$ in the past (by using an appropriate time window). Furthermore, to obtain $\widehat{T_x(y)}^t$ Marsh proposes using the maximum value within the observed time-window, the minimum value, or the average. But how can one, for example, obtain the average value? The formula for the general trust average is given as follows (note that A denoted the set of all situations):

$$\widehat{T_x(y)} = \frac{1}{|A|} \sum_{\alpha \in A} T_x(y). \qquad (3.3)$$

As cooperation is supposed to be the main consequence of trust (again, trust is seen as a cooperation enabler), a cooperation threshold needs to be defined. This threshold provides the basis for judging whether cooperation between agents will occur or not:

$$CT_x(y, \alpha) = \frac{PR_x(\alpha)}{PC_x(y, \alpha) + \widehat{T_x(y)}} \cdot I_x(\alpha) \qquad (3.4)$$

In the above equation CT denotes the cooperation threshold, PR denotes perceived risk, and PC denotes perceived competence (the meaning of subscripts and arguments is the same as in the preceding text).

Having the so far developed formulae arsenal, Marsh was finally able to demonstrate how artificial agents societies can be used to evaluate trust in cooperation (strategies) through game-theory experiments.

Marsh paved the way for computational trust and reputation management by making a valuable contribution to the formalisation of trust and its computational support. But it should come as no surprise that his work also raised questions as to what trust actually is, whether it is independent of morality, ethics, and emotion, and whether it plays any role other than to promote cooperation. The points of his work that have left more questions than answers are the following: Are the values for measuring and expressing values of related variables really from the interval $[-1, 1]$, or would a more qualitative type of estimates be more accurate? Furthermore, are the chosen operators the most appropriate ones or not? Moreover, is the exclusion of the system dynamics view, where feed-back loops play an important role, acceptable (e.g. when an agent makes a trust related decision towards another agent, this decision affects the whole community, and this new state of the community further influences this very agent's trust dynamics)? It should be noted that Marsh himself realized that his model exhibits some problems when dealing with extreme values (e.g. value zero), and that there are additional problems when dealing with negative trust values and the propagation of such values.

3.1.2 Subjective Logic

Subjective logic is a formalism that has been often used in the field of trust. It is explained extensively in [18], but for the purpose of this section, its early development, described in [17], will serve as a basis.

Subjective logic is a calculus for subjective beliefs. These beliefs are about situations that involve uncertainty, where uncertainty can be a result of, e.g. incomplete knowledge. Consequently, this logic is a sensible attempt to model reasoning when it comes to trust. The core concept is the so called opinion ω and this opinion is represented as a triplet b, d, u denoting *belief*, *disbelief* and *uncertainty*. Each element of this triplet has a value assigned from the interval $[0, 1]$, while $b + d + u = 1$. So $\omega_p^A = (b, d, u)$ expresses agent's A belief in a certain binary statement p.

Suppose the statement p is "Alice *is worth* relying on to buy a good book and get the best offer on this book for me." This statement has to be considered as a binary statement, having a true or a false value. When it is spoken by Bob (denoted as B), it can be interpreted in terms of trust because its semantics clearly implies reliability trust.

Let us further assume that Bob says "Alice *is worth* relying on to buy a good car and get the best offer on this car for me." (this statement will be referred to as statement q). Using these two statements let's try to calculate Bob's trust for both cases together, so that reliance on Alice (denoted also as A) for buying a book and a car in the expected way is considered together. In such a case the conjunction operator can be applied. Let Bob's opinion about binary statement p be given as $\omega_p^B = (b_p^B, d_p^B, u_p^B)$, while his opinion about statement q be given as $\omega_q^B = (b_q^B, d_q^B, u_q^B)$. Now Bob's opinion about p and q both being true is given by

$$\omega_{p \wedge q}^B = \omega_p^B \wedge \omega_q^B =$$
$$= (b_p^B b_q^B, \; d_p^B + d_q^B - d_p^B d_q^B, \; b_p^B u_q^B + u_p^B b_q^B + u_p^B u_q^B). \tag{3.5}$$

To provide a concrete example, let $\omega_p^B = (0.7, 0.2, 0.1)$ and let $\omega_q^B = (0.8, 0.2, 0)$. This means that $\omega_{p \wedge q}^B = (0.56, 0.36, 0.08)$.

Assume now that Cindy contacts Bob and asks him about Alice's trustworthiness in terms of buying a book on behalf of another person. The statement p provided by Bob is his opinion to be used together with Cindy's opinion to obtain a consensus. Subjective algebra also provides operators for such cases, and one appropriate operator in this case is the *consensus operator*. Put another way, this operator gives trust values considering Bob and Cindy as a new, aggregated entity (i.e. as a group). So let Bob's opinion be $\omega_p^B = (b_p^B, d_p^B, u_p^B)$, and Cindy's opinion be $\omega_p^C = (b_p^C, d_p^C, u_p^C)$. Then their consensus (group) opinion is

$$\omega_p^{B,C} = \omega_p^B \oplus \omega_p^C =$$
$$= (b_p^{B,C}, \quad d_p^{B,C}, \quad u_p^{B,C}),$$

where

$$b_p^{B,C} = (b_p^B u_p^C + b_p^C u_p^B)/(u_p^B + u_p^C - u_p^B u_p^C),$$
$$d_p^{B,C} = (d_p^B u_p^C + d_p^C u_p^B)/(u_p^B + u_p^C - u_p^B u_p^C),$$
$$u_p^{B,C} = (u_p^B u_p^C)/(u_p^B + u_p^C - u_p^B u_p^C).$$

(3.6)

Operators introduced by subjective logic can be uniquely mapped to the Beta PDF (probability density function), thus preserving a sound mathematical basis, one of the main benefits of this formalism for modelling trust. It is evident that it also suitable for machine-based processing.

However, the key question is whether humans, when it comes to trust, really function according to the premises and conclusions of this logic. Furthermore, a deep understanding of the underlying operations in subjective logic is likely beyond the comprehension of ordinary users of IT services. However, the line of reasoning behind this logic is appealing, at least within the research community, which is proven by the fact that it has gained a lot of interest there.

3.1.3 Qualitative Assessment Dynamics (QAD)

Qualitative Assessment Dynamics (QAD) was introduced some 15 years ago and since then has evolved from an algebraic semi-group into a formal structure of its own [41–43]. QAD operators and operands have linguistic roots and closely reflect common-sense reasoning when it comes to modelling trust. Consequently, their underlying semantics can be intuitively comprehended by humans.

In QAD, trust is treated in a rather straightforward way. Whatever trust is (be the result of a purely rational decision-making process, or just a simple emotional state), it can be abstractly seen as a relationship between a trustor (i.e. entity that is trusting) and a trustee (i.e. entity that is being trusted). This relation can be represented as a

Fig. 3.2 An example of
society with trust assessments

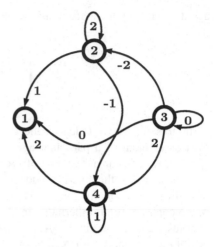

graph with two nodes, trustor and trustee, and the relationship between these two
nodes denoted by a directed arc.

Using this approach, a society with n agents can be modelled with a directed
graph with n nodes that is referred to as *trust graph*. The arcs in the trust graph
are weighted accordingly. Their weights are qualitative, because QAD discerns
five levels of assessments when it comes to trust: totally trusted, partially trusted,
undecided, partially distrusted, and totally distrusted. These levels of assessments
are represented as 2, 1, 0, −1, −2, respectively.[1] In addition, if an assessment is not
known, it is denoted by a hyphen, "-".

As graphs can be equivalently represented by matrices, the general form of such
a society with n agents can be shown by trust matrix **A** (in this matrix the element
$a_{i,j}$ denotes the trust of agent i towards agent j):

$$\mathbf{A} = \begin{pmatrix} a_{11} & a_{12} & \dots & a_{1n} \\ a_{21} & a_{22} & \dots & a_{2n} \\ \vdots & \vdots & \ddots & \vdots \\ a_{n1} & a_{n2} & \dots & a_{nn} \end{pmatrix} \tag{3.7}$$

Suppose we have a society of four agents and their assessments as shown in
Fig. 3.2. Then the corresponding trust (assessment) matrix is given in Eq. (3.8).
From this matrix we can see that agent number one is an agent that does not want to
disclose its assessments, or it may be a dumb agent (e.g. a technological artefact).
Furthermore, the first element in the second row denotes that agent 2 partially trusts

---

[1] Although these assessments seem to form a Likert scale, this is not the case. Such particular kind
of ordered categorical data is referred to as a semantic differential scale.

agent 1, but fully trusts itself, and so on.

$$
\mathbf{A} = \begin{pmatrix} \overset{-}{1} & \overset{-}{2} & \overset{-}{-} & \overset{-}{-1} \\ 0 & -2 & 0 & 2 \\ 2 & - & - & 1 \end{pmatrix}
\tag{3.8}
$$

In trust matrix A (such as the one given in Eq. (3.8)), row values state the trust assessment of a particular agent towards other agents in a society (e.g. the second row gives an assessment of agent two related to the other agents in society). Columns, on the other hand, provide society assessments related to a particular agent (e.g. the second column gives an assessment of agent 2 provided by the other agents in the community). Furthermore, in an assessment of matrix $\mathbf{A}$ the k-th trust vector denotes the k-th column, i.e. $\mathbf{A}_{n,k} = (\alpha_{1,k}, \alpha_{2,k}, \ldots, \alpha_{n,k})$, while the k-th trust sub-vector denotes the vector $\underline{\mathbf{A}}_{n,k} = (\alpha_{n1,k}, \alpha_{2,k}, \ldots, \alpha_{n1,k})$, where all unknown values are excluded from the k-th trust vector $\mathbf{A}_{n,k}$—the ordering of the remaining n_1 non-unknown values remains unchanged.

It is now possible to introduce some key operators. If the initial, pre-operation value is not known (the pre-operation value is denoted by "-"), then this assessment remains unknown also after the operation (the post-operation value is denoted by "+"). If the initial value is known, then the post-operation value is obtained according to the selected operator as follows (note that the value of n_1 is the value obtained by subtracting the number of undefined assessments from n):

$\alpha_{ij}^- \neq$ " $-$ " :

$\Uparrow_j$: $max(\alpha_{1,i}^-, \alpha_{2,i}^-, \ldots, \alpha_{j,i}^-, \ldots, \alpha_{n,i}^-) \rightarrow \alpha_{j,i}^+$; $(i = 1, 2, \ldots, n_1)$ (3.9)

$\Downarrow_j$: $min(\alpha_{1,i}^-, \alpha_{2,i}^-, \ldots, \alpha_{j,i}^-, \ldots, \alpha_{n,i}^-) \rightarrow \alpha_{j,i}^+$; $(i = 1, 2, \ldots, n_1)$ (3.10)

$$
\Uparrow_j: \begin{cases} \alpha_{j,i}^- \rightarrow \alpha_{j,i}^+ & if\ \frac{1}{n_1}\sum_{i=1}^{n_1}\alpha_{i,k}^- \leq \alpha_{j,i}^- \\ \\ \alpha_{j,i}^- \rightarrow \left\lfloor \alpha_{j,i}^+ + 1 \right\rfloor & otherwise \end{cases}
\tag{3.11}
$$

$$
\Downarrow_j: \begin{cases} \alpha_{j,i}^- \rightarrow \alpha_{j,i}^+ & if\ \frac{1}{n_1}\sum_{i=1}^{n_1}\alpha_{i,k}^- \geq \alpha_{j,i}^- \\ \alpha_{j,i}^- \rightarrow \left\lfloor \alpha_{j,i}^+ - 1 \right\rfloor & otherwise \end{cases}
\tag{3.12}
$$

$$\leadsto_j: \begin{cases} \left[\frac{1}{n_1}\sum_{i=1}^{n_1}\alpha_{i,k}^-\right] \to \alpha_{j,i}^+ & \text{if } \frac{1}{n_1}\sum_{i=1}^{n_1}\alpha_{i,k}^- < 0 \\ \left[\frac{1}{n_1}\sum_{i=1}^{n_1}\alpha_{i,k}^-\right] \to \alpha_{j,i}^+ & \text{otherwise} \end{cases} \tag{3.13}$$

$$\leftrightarrow_j: \begin{cases} \left[\frac{1}{n_1}\sum_{i=1}^{n_1}\alpha_{i,k}^-\right] \to \alpha_{j,i}^+ & \text{if } \frac{1}{n_1}\sum_{i=1}^{n_1}\alpha_{i,k}^- > 0 \\ \left[\frac{1}{n_1}\sum_{i=1}^{n_1}\alpha_{i,k}^-\right] \to \alpha_{j,i}^+ & \text{otherwise} \end{cases} \tag{3.14}$$

$$\updownarrow_j: \quad random(-2,-1,0,1,2) \to \alpha_{j,i}^+; \qquad (i = 1, 2, \ldots, n_1) \tag{3.15}$$

$$\alpha_{ij}^- = \text{``}-\text{''}:$$
$$\alpha_{j,i}^- \to \text{``}-\text{''} \tag{3.16}$$

The names of these operators are expressive enough to reflect the nature of their operations, and are as follows (from top to the bottom): extreme optimistic assessment (EOA), extreme pessimistic assessment (EPA), moderate optimistic assessment (MOA), moderate pessimistic assessment (MPA), centralist (consensus seeking) assessment (CSA), non-centralistic assessment (NCA), and assessment hoping (AH).

To illustrate QAD in action we will study the dynamics of the example given in Fig. 3.2. Let us assume that the chosen agents are governed by the following operators: agent 1 has no operator, because this is a so called dumb agent (i.e. an agent that does not, or cannot, disclose its trust assessments), agent 2 is governed by an EOA operator, agent 3 is governed by a CSA operator, and agent 4 by an MPA operator. Starting with the trust values as given in the above mentioned figure, and following the assigned operators, in the next two steps the trust dynamics in this society will look as shown in Fig. 3.3.

The graphs shown in Fig. 3.3 capture the dynamics of trust assessments as a result of interactions among agents. New assessments of a particular agent are based on its own assessments, assessments of other agents, and the operator that defines how this particular agent is processing these assessments.

The strong point of QAD is that it takes into account that humans are not only rational, but in a significant number of cases and contexts a bounded rationality can, at most, be assumed (while in some cases even irrationality takes place [37]). Furthermore, QAD performs very well when compared to other trust management solutions even in settings where defeating agents exist [16, 45]. Last but not least, QAD is not computationally intensive, so it is applicable to a wide range of domains [38]. Its main weakness is the mapping of qualitative differential scale values to quantitative ones to enable the use of its operators, which is likely not generally applicable to human reasoning.

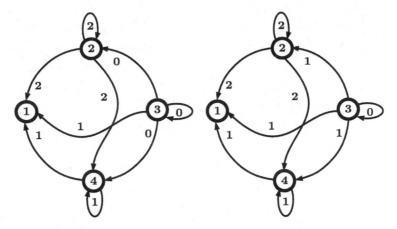

Fig. 3.3 The example society and its trust dynamics

3.1.4 Other Methods

This subsection presents solutions that are often termed as trusted technologies. It is important that a clear distinction between computational trust management solutions and these trusted technologies be made. Trusted technologies could be best described as trust enabling technologies as they do not deal with trust itself, but rather lead to implementations which have trust-related properties. Among these indirectly trust enabling technologies two core (and most important) types should be mentioned:

- The first types are traditional security and privacy provisioning systems that range from access control systems (an early example is described in [27]), while more recent examples can be found in [29] and [3]) to security services providing solutions based on cryptography (these are extensively described in many places such as [39]). This is a kind of technology that has been around for decades, the main characteristics of which is the intensive deployment of traditional cryptographic mechanisms and services.
- The second types are the rising star among bankers, governments, etc. These are block-chain technologies that serve to implement contemporary ledger solutions. They are based on BitCoin technology and deploy the so called proof of work for providing integrity (and partially authentication) of groups of transactions. This proof of work is collaboratively calculated and verified by the distributed community of hundreds or thousands of users, which makes it hard to forge. It is calculated for each block of transactions, and when a new block is formed it is cryptographically linked to existing ones, and a new proof of work is generated. More details about block-chain ledgers can be found in [14], for example.

However, even if an entity is using trusted technology this does not mean that this entity (or its service) can be trusted. BitCoin, for example, is often linked to dark-net and illegal transactions.

3.2 Reputation Management Systems Methods and Models

Contrary to trust management systems, which provide an insight into trust dynamics within an agent or society of agents, reputation management systems deal more with outer manifestations (i.e. the face values of expressed opinions) and their distribution. The line between the two kinds of systems is thin. In fact, once a pure trust management system is extended to support the propagation of assessments (by enabling the sharing of trust values among agents) then this system becomes a reputation system. Therefore, this section focuses on those systems where the propagation of assessments (opinions) core activity.

Reputation, according to the Cambridge English Dictionary, is defined as "the opinion that people in general have about someone or something, or how much respect or admiration someone or something receives, based on past behaviour or character" [5]. In the Merriam-Webster Dictionary it is defined as "the common opinion that people have about someone or something; the way in which people think of someone or something" [23].

In line with these definitions we will define reputation management as *procedures regarding the selective exposure of personal information and activities in order to shed light on how people function in networks when establishing credentials, building trust with others, and gathering information to make decisions* [31]. Consequently, *a reputation management system will be defined as a technological artefact that supports and automates reputation management.*

So reputation systems serve as facilitators of trust. To do this as successfully as possible, one key requirement is support for anonymity—and right this requirement for supporting anonymous transactions is also the Achille's heel of reputation systems as it enables numerous forms of misbehaviour [32]. Despite the requirement of anonymity, collecting, distributing and aggregating information about the users' behaviour is the means of generally ensuring the intended functionality of such systems.

Resnick et al. observe three important elements related to misbehaviour [32]. First comes the dilemma as to whether an interaction is a one-shot interaction or a long term one (the first one, especially among strangers, provides more grounds for uncooperative behaviour). Second, one has to be convinced of the other party's abilities and dispositions in a given context (which may change with time). Third, if this is to be a long-term relationship, reciprocation (cooperation) comes into the process more strongly. Therefore past behaviour plays a vital role, foreshadowing the agent's present (and future) trustworthiness. Consequently, reputation systems have to fulfil (at minimum) three properties: entities have to be long-lived (so that past behaviour can play a role), feedbacks have to be captured and distributed (if needed, after appropriate processing), and these feed-backs have to be taken into account by users.

These requirements can be considered as inherent ones, implying required functionalities for reputation systems. Achieving them is not a trivial task. The first thing is to obtain feed-back and there are notable problems with giving appropriate incentives for users to do so. Next, even when feed-back is obtained, positive values usually exceed negative ones, e.g. due to the fear of retaliatory actions. And lastly, distributing valid feed back may still be a challenge, as various schemes have to be presented to users in a meaningful and understandable way.

3.2.1   eBay Reputation System

The Feedback Forum of eBay is among the most well-known, the oldest and probably simplest reputation systems (which does not mean that its efficiency and usability is to be questioned).

This system accumulates ratings for a given member that are provided by other members for a particular transaction. The feedback may be negative (-1), neutral (0), or positive ($+1$). When a member earns enough ratings she is assigned an appropriate star level, starting with yellow (from 10 to 49 ratings), continuing with blue (from 50 to 99) and going all the way to the silver shooting star (having at least one million ratings). A complete feed-back thus provides the number of transactions (star mark) and the accumulated experiences rating (e.g. 95% positive ratings), as well as the exact numbers of positive, neutral and negative ratings.

Amazon and other widely known service providers use similar systems, which may vary in their rating scales (e.g. ratings from 1 to 5 or from 1 to 10) and in recording additional attributes such as prompt response, friendliness of buyers and sellers, using averages instead of absolute values, and so on. These systems share a common feature of not inherently dealing with false feed-backs, even though their operators deploy strategies in the background to minimize them.

The main advantage of these systems is that they are easy to implement and are so ubiquitous that almost every user nowadays is familiar with them. However, the drawback is that their aggregates provide rather rough measures with many potentially useful pieces of information missing, such as context. Furthermore, despite their simplicity, the semantics are rather unclear, so providing, for example, a mapping between eBay's and Amazon's systems is not a straightforward procedure.

3.2.2 Mui's Reputation Model

Mui's reputation model is among the earlier works in this area and focuses on agents based simulation environments [25].[2] He provides an overview of the area, and although also trust management systems are mentioned, his contribution belongs more in the area of reputation systems. Mui gives an analysis of the properties of reputation, which he refers to as reputation typology. This typology comprises the following elements:

- Granularity—there are individual and group reputation, where the first one is about a particular agent, and the latter is about an aggregated entity of individual agents.
- Personalisation—reputation is usually about how an agent is viewed in the eyes of other agents relative to its social network, while another kind of reputation, a global one, is not tied to any social network (as is the case with ratings on eBay and so on).
- Contextualisation—reputation is not a general category, but it is tied to a particular context (or contexts).
- Nature of origin—direct and indirect reputation exist, where direct reputation is based on direct encounters (which may involve direct acts or just direct observations), while indirect reputation is based on second-hand evidence. In this latter case it may be prior-derived (e.g. in form of prejudices), group derived (e.g. when an agent's reputation is based on the reputation of a group to which it belongs to) and propagated (which is similar to word of mouth).

Mui's model is probabilistic and based on Bayesian statistics [26]. The reputation of an agent is inferred through propagated ratings from evaluations of the agent's neighbours. These propagated ratings are also weighted by the reputation of these same neighbours.

Reputation is formalized by introducing a set of agents $A = \{a_1, a_2, \ldots, a_m\}$ and a set of objects $O = \{o_1, o_2, \ldots, o_n\}$. These agents provide ratings ρ which may be approve (also denoted as 1), and disapprove (also denoted 0):

$$\rho : A \times O \rightarrow \{0, 1\} \tag{3.17}$$

Once having a rating $\rho_{i,j}$, which denotes the rating of object o_j provided by agent a_i, its propagation process can start taking place. This process is carried out through an encounter e that is an element of the set of all encounters E:

$$e \in E, \ E = A^2 \times O \times \{0, 1\} \cup \{\bot\} \tag{3.18}$$

---

[2]Mui's formalism and QAD were developed independently, albeit roughly at the same time, and although they differ at their cores, it is interesting to note that they introduced some similar concepts [43].

Following this equation, an encounter between agents a_i and a_j, where the first agent consults the second one of an object o_k (the latter being evaluated as approved by the second agent) is denoted as $e = \{a_i, a_j, o_k, 1\}$.

Let us assume a simplified case, where only uniform contexts are taken into account. Before interacting with an object o_k agent a_i asks other agents for their ratings of o_k. Where the weighted sum of other agents' ratings is greater than a threshold t_i, the interaction takes place. Thus, the weights are assigned in line with the level of approval of another agent a_j from the viewpoint of a_i.

Finally, we will define reputation R as the probability that in the next encounter a_j's rating about a new object will be approved by a_i. Defining a_i's approval of itself to be 1, reputation is given by the mapping

$$R : A \times A \rightarrow [0, 1]. \tag{3.19}$$

The notion of a state S for the system as a whole is also needed (in the case of a uniform context, it holds that $S = R$), as well as the inclusion of the history h, which is an element of the set H of all histories, resulting in the mapping:

$$h : T \rightarrow S \times E, \tag{3.20}$$

where the set of time increments is $T = \{0, 1, \ldots, t\}$.

The reputation of an agent in the eyes of others changes through encounters with this agent, and after each encounter agent's a_j reputation in the eyes of agent a_i results in a new state S' of the system ($newstate : S \times E \rightarrow S'$).

Now, to enable inferences based on second hand evidence, let ρ denote the rating that the j-th agent reports to agent i about object k. By introducing a reputation propagation function f the actual rating of the object by agent a_i based on the indirect data will be $\rho_{i,k} = f(\rho_{i,j}, \rho_{j,k})$. The concrete nature of the propagation function f can be based on a centrality, preference based one, and Bayesian inference based one.

Mui's formalism also relies on representing societies with graphs where the edges between the vertices are weighted with reputation values. Suppose that a certain society consists of the three agents and reputation assessments shown in Fig. 3.4. This society can be equivalently represented by the corresponding adjacency matrix

Fig. 3.4 An example society graph with propagation weights on its links

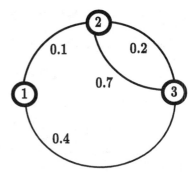

given in Eq. (3.21) (it is assumed that agents fully agree with their own judgements, so the diagonal elements in this matrix are always 1):

$$\mathbf{A} = \begin{pmatrix} 1 & 0.1 & 0 \\ 0 & 1 & 0.7 \\ 0.4 & 0.2 & 1 \end{pmatrix} \tag{3.21}$$

With all the apparatus presented so far it is possible to introduce reputation rating x_i of agent i, where obtaining a new reputation value x_i for agent i is done by summing the weighted ratings of the whole society:

$$x_i^+ = a_{1i}x_1^- + a_{2i}x_2^- + \ldots + a_{ni}x_n^- \tag{3.22}$$

Assuming a community as shown in Fig. 3.4, and assuming further that for agent 1 the reputation measure is 1, for agent 2 it is 0.8, and for agent 3 it is again 1, then the rating process for agent 3 is

$$x_3^+ = a_{13}x_1^- + a_{23}x_2^- + a_{33}x_3^- = 0 * 1 + 0.7 * 0.8 + 1 * 1 = 1.56. \tag{3.23}$$

Beside the above kind of rating of one member by the community, which is referred to as centrality based rating, Mui also introduces variants like preference-based rating, where the preferences of each member are taken into account when selecting the reputable members that are most likely to be approved, etc.

In summary, Mui's formalism is another kind of straightforward reputation management model, in which the basic underlying operations are easy to comprehend. On the other hand, its weakness is the lack of evidence that the proposed propagation model reflects reality.

3.2.3 Reputation Model by Yu and Singh

Yu and Singh's model views reputation as the cumulative belief of a group of agents about another agent, assuming that every agent involved does not know with full certainty the trustworthiness (or untrustworthiness) of the rest of the agents. As a solution, agents can estimate the degree of trust about other agents.

To deal with this uncertainty the Dempster Shafer theory of evidence has proven very useful. This theory was developed in the 1960s an 1970s, and has garnered a lot of interest along with further advances over the years [44]. This theory presents an extension of Bayesian statistics and it starts with a frame of discernment called Θ that represents all atomic states in an observed domain. Using this set, a basic probability assignment (also called belief mass) is performed: $m : 2^{\Theta} \rightarrow [0, 1]$, where $m\{\} = 0$ and $\sum_{A \subseteq \Theta} m(A) = 1$ (a belief mass $m_{\Theta}(A)$ expresses the belief assigned to the whole set A without expressing any belief in its subsets).

The next definition introduces the belief function $b(A)$, which is defined as the sum of the beliefs committed to the possibilities in A. These possibilities include appropriate subsets of A, but when not all of these subsets are taken into account, there remain subsets with an empty intersection with the former subsets, which can be interpreted as a disbelief, or $d(A)$.

The rest of the remaining subsets can be interpreted as uncertainty, which is reflected in the below definition:

$$b(x) = \sum_{y \subseteq x} m(y), \quad d(x) = \sum_{x \cap y = \emptyset} m(y), \quad u(x) = \sum_{y \nsubseteq x, \, x \cap y \neq \emptyset} m(y);$$

$$b, d, u \in [0, 1], \qquad b(x) + d(x) + u(x) = 1, \qquad x, y \in 2^{\Theta} \tag{3.24}$$

For example, let the frame of discernment Θ consist of atomic states x_1, x_2, x_3, x_4, x_5, and two non-atomic states, $x_6 = \{x_1, x_2, x_3\}$ and $x_7 = \{x_3, x_4, x_5\}$. Then belief in x_6 is the sum of the belief masses assigned to x_1, x_2 and x_3, while disbelief assigned to this set is the sum of the belief masses in states x_4 and x_5 (i.e. sets that have an empty intersection with x_6). Consequently, the uncertainty of x_6 is the sum of belief masses on sets x_7 and Θ. This sample situation is illustrated in Fig. 3.5.

Yu and Singh use this theory as a basis for reputation dynamics, while starting everything with trust T, so that the frame of discernment is $\Theta = \{T\}, \{\neg T\}, \{T, \neg T\}$. When an agent is evaluating the trustworthiness of another agent, uncertainty can be added, e.g. $m(\{T\}) = 0.7$, $m(\{\neg T\}) = 0$, and $m(\{T, \neg T\}) = 0.3$ (note that these belief masses can be interpreted as belief, disbelief and uncertainty). When additional evidence becomes available, this agent may increase his estimate of trustworthiness, i.e. 0.7, and reduce accordingly the undecided value, e.g. $m(\{T\}) = 0.8$, $m(\{\neg T\}) = 0$, and $m(\{T, \neg T\}) = 0.2$. Or, if future evidence supports this, the currently undecided value can be added to untrustworthiness, so the result will be $m(\{T\}) = 0.7$, $m(\{\neg T\}) = 0.3$, and $m(\{T, \neg T\}) = 0$.

Now reputation can be addressed. Suppose one agent evaluates the trustworthiness of another agent. The former agent's evaluation is based on direct observation and indirect observations in terms of belief ratings (also called referrals) given by other agents in a society (also called witnesses). The core question is now how to properly combine these referrals to obtain reputation.

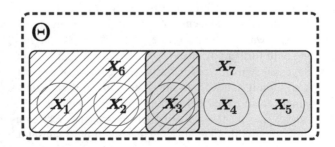

Fig. 3.5 An example set for the derivation of values for b, d and u

When agent A_r wants to evaluate the trustworthiness of agent A_g it first has to collect the referrals $r_1, r_2, \ldots, r_n$ from neighbouring agents $A_1, A_2, \ldots, A_n$. Then agent A_g constructs a graph and appends each referral to this graph. When appending the referral the trustworthiness of the witnesses themselves is included. And it is where the belief function (as introduced by the theory of evidence) comes into play. The so called orthogonal sum of beliefs is used, denoted as $b_1 \oplus b_2$. How is this operation performed? Let $b_1 = 0.8$, $d_1 = 0$, $u_1 = 0.2$ and $b_2 = 0.9$, $d_2 = 0$, $u_2 = 0.1$, then

	b_2	u_2
b_1	0.72	0.08
u_1	0.18	0.02

Finally, $b_{12} = 0.72 + 0.18 + 0.08 = 0.98$, $d_{12} = 0$, and $u_{12} = 0.02$.

Now suppose agent A_g has witness A_{w_i}, and this witness has associated referrals $r_1, r_2, \ldots, r_k$. Then the cumulative belief for witness A_{w_i} is obtained as

$$b(r_i) = b(r_1) \oplus b(r_2) \oplus \ldots \oplus b(r_k). \tag{3.25}$$

Now the reputation *rep* of the witness A_{w_i} can be introduced as

$$rep(A_{w_i}) = b(\{T_{w_i}\}). \tag{3.26}$$

The formalism proposed by Yu and Singh is closely fitted to the Dempster Shaffer theory of evidence and therefore not easily comprehended by ordinary users. Although it is true that the Yu and Singh formalism has been developed for use in artificial agents environments, our goal is to support humans in e-environments. Its strong point, however, is its solid mathematical basis, so it is a good candidate for scientific simulations.

3.2.4 Beta Reputation System

The beta reputation system belongs to Bayesian systems. It takes binary ratings (like trusted, distrusted) as inputs and continuously updates the Beta probability density function (Beta PDF) [19]. A new reputation score is obtained by combining the previous score with the new rating.

The basis for this system is the fact that a posteriori probabilities of binary events can be given with beta distributions. Their probability density functions (PDFs) belong to a family of density functions that are indexed by parameters α and β

(the restriction is that $p \neq 0$ if $\alpha < 1$, and $p \neq 1$ if $\beta < 1$):

$$Beta(p|\alpha,\beta) = \frac{\Gamma(\alpha+\beta)}{\Gamma(\alpha)\Gamma(\beta)}p^{\alpha-1}(1-p)^{\beta-1}$$

$$\alpha, \beta > 0, \quad 0 \leq p \leq 1.$$

(3.27)

The probability expectation of beta distribution is $E(p) = \alpha/(\alpha+\beta)$. But how can this be linked to trust?

Assuming a binary event, suppose that the number of positive outcomes of interactions with some agent is r, and the number of negative outcomes is s. The corresponding beta function is then obtained by setting $\alpha = r+1$ and $\beta = s+1$ (if so, then in cases where no positive or negative experiences are known, the beta is given by $\alpha = 1$ and $\beta = 1$). Now when r positive experiences are obtained, and s negative ones, the Beta PDF parameters are: $\alpha = r+1$ and $\beta = s+1$. So, in a case where there are five positive experiences and three negative ones the expectation probability is $E(p) = 0.6$. As suggested in [19], the interpretation of this value is that future outcomes are certainly uncertain, but the relative frequency of positive (trusted) outcomes is most likely 0.6.

Based on these formal considerations a reputation system can be defined by introducing reputation function φ. Let r_T^X and s_T^X state the collective amount of positive and negative feedbacks about agent T provided by atomic or non-atomic agent (i.e. an aggregation of agents) X. Then the reputation function is obtained as

$$\varphi(p|r_T^X, s_T^X) = \frac{\Gamma(r_T^X + s_T^X + 2)}{\Gamma(r_T^X + 1)\Gamma(s_T^X + 1)}p^{r_T^X}(1-p)^{s_T^X},$$

$$0 \leq p \leq 1, \ 0 \leq r_T^X, \ 0 \leq s_T^X.$$

(3.28)

The probability expectation of the reputation function is given as follows:

$$E(\varphi(p|r_T^X, s_T^X)) = (r_T^X + 1)/(r_T^X + r_T^S + 2).$$

(3.29)

The interpretation of function φ is analogous to that given above for Beta PDF, while the arguments in the reputation function (when compared to the ordinary beta PDF) are interpreted a bit differently to reflect the e-business reality. Actually, experiences in e-business are not binary events, but are more likely to be degrees of satisfaction r and dissatisfaction s, where r and s are better utilized when having continuous values.

As with Subjective logic, in order to reflect the dynamics of reputation in a society, appropriate operators are introduced for combining feedbacks in reputation functions, discounting them, and so on. This is one major advantage of the beta reputation system. Another advantage is its strong mathematical basis, although its weakness is certainly its high degree of complexity, which makes it very difficult for the average person to comprehend. In addition, it is not clear whether (or how well) it reflects the dynamics of real human societies when it comes to trust.

3.2.5   ReGreT

The ReGreT system aims to provide reputation management on the basis of interpreting reputation as an opinion (or view) of one agent about something, where this something can be another agent, a technological solution, etc. [35]. The model divides reputation into individual, social, and (interestingly) ontological. While individual reputation is about judgements in case of direct interaction between the evaluating and the evaluate agent, the lack of such interactions leads to inclusion of judgements of other agents in a society, which represents social dimension. The last, ontological trust, refers to the multifaceted nature of reputation and is introduced to capture the context details of a certain opinion [34].

The core of the ReGreT system consists of three knowledge bases. The first one is the interactions outcomes database. The second one is the information database, where information from other sources is stored. The third one is the database that stores the graphs that define an agent's social view of the community, and is referred to as the socio-grams database. These three databases comprise the infrastructural core of ReGreT. They are loaded with information from two modules (and these modules reflect ReGreT's clear distinction between trust and reputation):

- The direct trust module processes direct experiences and their contributions to trust calculation.
- The reputation module cares about "second-hand" values and is specialized into three areas: witness reputation (as the name implies, these are data provided by witnesses that are used in trust calculation), neighbourhood reputation (which uses data extracted from social relationships), and system reputation (which provides data based on the roles and general properties of an observed agent).

The above data are then used by an inference module that deploys an ontological point of view. They are considered in such a way that supports seeing reputation (and trust) as a multi-faceted concept, but it is still possible to come to a single trust and reputation value. ReGreT calculates values in a very flexible way using all kinds of information, e.g. an agent may prefer system reputation sources over neighbourhood information, and so on. Furthermore, these data also have associated reliability measures to additionally support agents by showing how confident a certain value is (from the system point of view).

As mentioned, ReGreT builds on three dimensions of reputation, the individual dimension, the social dimension and the ontological dimension:

- The individual dimension is about direct interaction among agents and is considered to be the most reliable. It is tied to an outcome of an interaction that is about a particular course of an action and its actual result. Elements of an outcome result in a reputation type with list of issues. Each issue is identified together with the details about how it affects reputation. When deriving the final outcome reputation, recent outcomes are given higher weights and all the outcomes are then averaged. In addition, the number of outcomes is taken into account when deciding about the final outcome reputation.
- The social dimension complements the individual dimension and is important in first encounters with another agent or with newcomers. The social reputation can be witness reputation, neighbourhood reputation or system reputation. Witness reputation is the shared beliefs about other members (aka witnesses) of a society. But they pose a danger of being biased or they may be false, not disclosed or overstated. To obtain witness information, the set of witnesses is identified first and grouped accordingly to minimize the effect of correlated evidence. Next, the received information is aggregated to obtain a single witness reputation value, which includes an appropriate degree of importance and reliability. Fuzzy rules play a central role here. To get more reliable scores from the social structure the antecedent of each rule is the type and the degree of a social interaction, while the consequence is the reliability of the information from the social relationship point of view.
- The ontological dimension focuses on a single behavioural aspect that a particular trust value is about. It enables the combination of various aspects to obtain the result for a particular aspect (the ontological dimension is modelled with graphs). Suppose that an agent is a swindler. Then this will influence its properties if acting as a seller, e.g. the property of overcharging will be given a higher positive weight, while service quality will be given a higher negative weight.

When forming the final opinion, the priority of dimensions (from the highest to the lowest) is as follows: individual dimension, social dimension, ontological dimension. In the absence (or uncertainty) of one dimension, other dimensions can be given higher weight.

ReGreT represents a fuzzy methods based reputation model (such an approach is used also in AFRAS [6] and Al Mutairi's approach [2]). It considers reputation and trust as linguistically fuzzy concepts, and therefore fuzzy logic is deployed to provide the necessary rules. Consequently, the result is the degree to which an agent can be considered as trustworthy or not trustworthy. These are the strong points of ReGreT. Another strong point is the elaboration of various facets of reputation (and trust) through the three dimensions. Its weak point is that it is rather complex to implement, and is particularly intended for artificial agents environments.

3.2.6   Some Other Approaches

The number of proposed and implemented computational reputation management models is still growing. While we have so far focused on the most typical types of models and described them in more detail, the ones that will be briefly presented in this subsection are those that have played an important role in the evolution of this domain (the basis for these descriptions is [36] and the respective original papers).

- **Abdul-Rahman and Hailes System**—Abdul-Rahman and Hailes have focused on reputation as a kind of social control of trust propagation [1]. So the authors start their work by analysing trust, but the emphasis is on its propagation throughout a society. In their case the "word-of-mouth" principle is the main reputation propagation mechanism among agents.

  This model uses four degrees of belief: very trustworthy, trustworthy, untrustworthy and very untrustworthy. An agent collects a tuple of past experiences for each other agent, and for each context. Before starting an interaction, the trust value is set to the maximal value in the tuple. In cases where more than one element in a tuple has the maximum value, an uncertainty is assigned. This uncertainty covers three possibilities: the case where good situations outnumber bad ones, the case where bad situations outnumber good ones, and the case where good situations equal bad ones.

  The problem with this formalism is that the range of values does not include the "I don't care" or "I don't know" cases, where an agent abstains from providing information (it may simply have never interacted with an agent that is being evaluated). The formalism has a tendency to select only the maximal values from tuples and also gives more importance to values coming from agents that have similar opinions and which need fewer adjustments. Furthermore, it evaluates only indirect trust, i.e. the one given by witnesses. At the same time, its strong point is that it provides support in those cases where there is a lack of reliable information. So an agent is able to estimate the reliability (i.e. trustworthiness) of another agent based on information gathered from the community.

- **Castelfranchi and Falcone Model**—This model is focused on the cognitive dimensions of trust [7]. The authors consider trust to play a key role in a context of delegation, as a kind of an agent's mental model of delegation. The core of this trust model can be described as a set of mental attitudes about a delegating agent who wants another agent to carry out an action, where the delegating agent believes that the delegated agent intends to carry out this action, and will persist in this effort.

  In order to lead to delegation, Castelfranchi and Falcone expose the antecedents like belief in the competence of the other agent, belief in dependence (i.e. so that the trustee has to be asked to perform a task on behalf of a trustor), and disposition belief (meaning that the trustee will do the desired task).

The main advantage of this model is the focus on the cognitive dimension of trust, while its limitation is its narrowing of the role of trust and reputation to delegated tasks only.

3.2.7 Complementary Approaches

Complementary approaches include those that serve the purpose of providing trust and reputation scores, but their methods of operation fall outside the scope of our definition of computational trust and reputation management system.

These approaches include services provided by consultation (business analytics) companies, and products and services evaluation organisations. Some of them pay attention to the internal operations of the observed business entities, while others consider purely the outer manifestations of the observed entities. The first kind of companies uses financial and related business data to perform risk analyses on selected organisations. Inputs like how well-managed and what kind of early defined operations a certain company has (with emphasis on consumer's issues like privacy protection and disputes resolutions) may be used. Standards like those from the International Standards Organisation (ISO) may be considered in these evaluations. The second kind of companies focuses only on products and services as such without paying attention to operations in the background that have resulted in particular products and services.

Some more visible representatives of the both kinds of companies are the following ones:

- The Better Business Bureau (https://www.bbb.org/) is an entity that "helps people find and recommend businesses, brands and charities they can trust." A company with a BBN rating system can be given an A+ through F rating. This rating is assigned by considering various factors such as the size of the company, its number of years in business, complaints management, and so on. According to [11], companies also get a profile when a consumer files a complaint, which is when BBN's arithmetic starts running that includes data about how the company responds to complaints and how it resolves them. However, organizations can also apply by themselves for BBB accreditation, but only after they reach grade B or higher, and accept BBB standards. There exist many similar services (Angie's List, Google+Local, etc.) and more details about them can be found in [11].
- International Consumer Research and Testing[3] is an international consortium for the facilitation of co-operation between its members organisations, which are focused on research and testing of consumer goods and services. These organisations usually have groups of reviewers and they provide ratings into their database(s), so other users are supposed to be able to make (more) informed

---

[3]http://www.international-testing.org/.

decisions about goods and services. Another example of an organisation in this category is BizRate.[4]

A rather specific kind of reputation measure is how a certain page on the web is ranking. The most-known algorithm for this kind of services is PageRank that provides the basis of operations for the web giant Google [28]. The core idea behind the algorithm is that the more one page is linked to by other pages, the more relevant it is. This ranking can provide a solid basis for the derivation of a certain page's reputation, or more precisely the information related to it. It should be noted that this information can involve many features such as the author of the page, the statements given on the page, the results provided by the page, and so on.

Although the above approaches do not belong to trust and reputation management systems, this does not mean that one can write them off. On the contrary, these services can play an important role in relation to computational trust and reputation management systems. The main issue is how to integrate them and to get the best of both worlds, which will be addressed in more detail in Chap. 4.

3.3 Evaluation of Trust Management and Reputation Models

A number of computational trust and reputation management methods and models have been proposed up to this point. It is natural to ask the following questions: Which model performs better than the others? Is there a model that performs better in one context while being worse in another context? Is there a clear overall winner among models?

Having an objective, quantitative evaluation is a key piece of information needed before deciding to implement a certain model in a concrete e-environment. No wonder that in the 1990s some approaches to evaluating models were done and so called test-beds were introduced. Among the earliest test-beds is the one described in [25], while more comprehensive ones have been introduced only recently. Two good examples are the Alfa TestBed [16] and the benchmarking system by Bidgoly and Ladani [4], while an extensive overview of the existing testbeds and their evaluation can be found in [20].

A detailed description of the Alfa TestBed (ATB) will be given in this chapter, because it has some important advantages compared to other test-beds.[5] Its main advantage is that the decision making process is taken into account when evaluating the various research methods and models. Why so?

The rationale for doing this is that trust and reputation can rarely be treated in isolation—sooner or later they become the basis for a certain action, be it for a direct interaction, or for providing an opinion to some third party, etc. Whenever

---

[4]http://www.bizrate.com/.

[5]The whole simulation environment can be freely downloaded from http://atb.fri.uni-lj.si/trac/browser/atb-code.

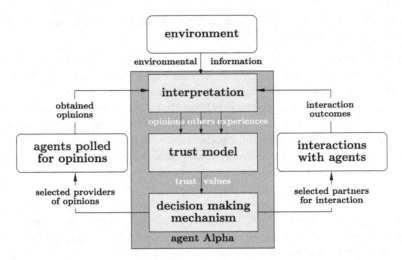

Fig. 3.6 Alpha test-bed architecture

an action is considered, a decision making process takes place. In certain test-beds decision-making is not taken into account at all. But in those cases where it is taken into account it is often assumed that if the same decision making mechanism is applied to all evaluated models then this somehow cancels out the influence of the decision making mechanism. Consequently, only the quality of trust (reputation) model remains evaluated. However, it turns out that this is not the case. A good decision making model can improve the performance of a bad trust model, while a good trust model can be degraded by a bad decision making model.

The architecture of ATB, which explicitly takes the decision-making process into account, is given in Fig. 3.6. ATB implements the following principles to evaluate a trust and reputation model:

- Agent Alpha (α) is running the tested trust model while other agents are being simulated.
- The ATB environment generates data that α conveys to its trust model that is currently being evaluated. The data consists of experiences from past interactions and opinions from other agents in the system.
- Afterwards, ATB evaluates the output of α's trust model, including the decisions that α makes.

So after receiving the environmental information, the α agent starts with the interpretation of these data, and obtains three kinds of interpreted streams: the first stream consists of agent's experiences, the second stream consists of others' opinions, while the third stream includes other information gathered from the environment.

These streams then drive the trust model under evaluation (e.g., Abdul-Rahman & Hailes or QAD) and appropriate trust values are calculated by α this way. These values now serve as an input to a selected decision making model and only then are actions taken by α agent. These actions can be of a two kinds: one line of action is "asking for further clarifications" (additional opinions), the other line is actions as such (i.e. interactions are starting to take place). The results of these two lines of actions then (together with other environmental information) close the loop at the information input part of α agent.

A detailed look at data structures used in the evaluation procedure conveys important information about the essence of ATB functioning:

- Agents—The central agent that evaluates a particular model is denoted as α. The set of all agents is denoted as A, while any other agent, except α, is denoted as a.
- Services—The set of services S consists of particular services s, which are considered in terms of interactions.
- Trust values—A trust value $\tau \in \Theta$ represents α's trust towards another particular agent, while Θ is the set of all trust values. Trust value is a tuple $\tau = < a, s, \omega >$, where $\omega \in \Omega$ represents the degree of trust towards a for a service s, while Ω is the set of all of these degrees. This is a kind of a weighting mechanism, because many models use weighting of trust opinions.
- Time—Time is a totally ordered set T of discrete time values, $\forall i : t_i \in T, t_i < t_{i+1}$.
- Experiences and assessments—A record of the interaction between α and some other agent a is called experience, ε, and is defined by a tuple $\varepsilon = < a, s, t, \lambda >$, where $\lambda \in \Lambda$ is α's assessment of a performance of service provider a for a service s at some time t. The set of all experiences is denoted as E.
- Opinions—An opinion $o \in O$ is a statement reported to α by some agent about another agent. Opinions are tuples $o = < a_o, a_p, s, t, \omega, u >$, where the trust degree ω is related to trust degree of a_o towards a_p at the time t, while additional element called uncertainty $u \in [0, 1]$ is given by a_0 to state the level of its uncertainty of the given trust degree.
- Trust model—The trust model is a particular computational model of trust that α is running as its own model, i.e. the one that is being simulated. Formally, a trust model is a function that maps a time value, a set of experiences, and a set of opinions to trust values: $T \times \mathcal{P}(E) \times \mathcal{P}(O) \longrightarrow \mathcal{P}(\Theta)$.

Using the above elements and data structures, the test-bed is started with a selected trust model. Now two kinds of evaluation scenarios can take place. In the first kind, trust models that do not have decision making mechanisms are evaluated, while in the second kind trust models with decision making mechanism are evaluated.

3.3.1 Models Without a Decision Making Mechanism

To start the interaction with other agents, ATB uses certain parameters so that these agents are properly selected. First, this makes sure that all models are evaluated independently from the decision making mechanism. Second, it assures that all models are evaluated using the same inputs. While the second reason is rather straightforward to understand, the first one needs some explanation. In cases where two trust models may compute two different trust values, even using the same decision making mechanism would lead to the selection of different partners. Consequently, different experiences would result, and these would be followed by different trust values, and so on. Therefore, the interactions are defined externally, by the ATB.

These are the steps of the evaluation protocol:

- For each new time increment, ATB triggers the model for a new iteration.
- ATB generates opinion tuples and submits them to the tested model.
- ATB chooses an interaction partner, generates an experience tuple, and submits this tuple to the model.
- The trust model under evaluation computes trust values and forwards them to ATB.
- ATB evaluates the received trust values.

3.3.2   Models with a Decision Making Mechanism

The evaluation protocol for models that have incorporated decision making mechanism has two modes. Mode A is for those decision making mechanisms that only select interaction partners, while mode B is for those models that also suggest whom to ask for an opinion. So let us have a look at mode A:

- For each new time increment, ATB triggers the model for a new iteration.
- ATB generates an opinion tuple and submits it to the tested model.
- The trust model that is being evaluated selects an agent for an interaction and reports this selection to the ATB.
- ATB generates an experience tuple for this selected agent and submits it to the trust model.
- The tested model computes the trust value and reports it to ATB.
- ATB evaluates the computed trust value and the utility obtained by this interaction.

Mode B has the same steps as given above, with an additional step appended. In this appended step, ATB evaluates the cost incurred by obtaining the requested opinions.

Now the data structures for the above protocols are needed. Agent α acquires experiences when having interactions with other agents that provide services. These services' quality reflects "the quality of agents". For an exact definition of the quality of agents and how interactions reflect them, new terms have to be given more precisely:

- The capability of an agent $a \in A$ for a service $s \in S$ at a time $t \in T$ represents an agent's ability and willingness to provide a quality service to agent α, which is expressed as a real number from $[0, 1]$, where 0 represents the lowest, and 1 the highest value: $A \times S \times T \rightarrow [0, 1]$.
- Every interaction is modelled by so called experience tuples, thus an experience tuple $\varepsilon = < a, s, t, \lambda >$ is a tuple where a denotes an agent a that α was interacting with for a service s of a type λ.

To create an experience, the testbed computes the outcome of an interaction from the capability of the agent that provides the service. In order to consider the realistic possibility that a particular outcome differs from the actual capability of the providing agent, a certain degree of randomness is added, but in such a way that in the long run the interaction outcomes reflect the actual agent's capabilities.

The last missing part is how ATB generates opinions, and how it addresses possible deceptions:

- An opinion is a tuple $o = < a_i, a_j, s, t, \omega, u >$, where ω denotes the trust degree of agent a_i towards agent a_j for a service s at time t, and where $u \in [0, 1]$ denotes uncertainty.
- Deception d is a mapping $d : [0, 1] \mapsto [0, 1]$, and this mapping is specific for a particular agent, where ATB operates with the following deception set values $D = \{d_t, d_c, d_{pe}, d_{ne}, d_r\}$. For each element in this set an exaggeration coefficient $\kappa \in [0, 1]$ is defined, so the actual deception models are as follows: for a truthful model $d_t(x) = x$, for a complementary model $d_c(x) = 1 - x$, for a positive exaggeration model $d_{pe}(x) = x(1 - \kappa) + \kappa$, for a negative exaggeration model $d_{ne}(x) = x(1 - \kappa)$, and for a random model $d_r = random(0, 1)$.

Deception is assigned to every agent in the system, and this is varied over time, from service to service and from agent to agent.

Before being able to evaluate a particular model, appropriate metrics have to be introduced. In the case of ATB, three metrics are proposed: accuracy, utility and opinion cost. Accuracy is concerned with how close a trust model gets in its assessments to the real capabilities of an agent. Utility involves α's relative performance when selecting quality interaction partners (the chosen interaction vs. those with the best qualities). Finally, cost is about efficiency of a decision making part (how much overhead it incurs in terms of additional communications, etc.).

Finally, having all the necessary elements in place, a particular simulation can be initialized and executed. For each simulation a so called scenario is determined that specifies the agent population, the assignment of capabilities, the assignment of deception models, the selection of partners and the selection of opinion providers.

After executing simulations, different results for the various trust models can be obtained. Thus, for example, the contrast between Abdul-Rahman & Hailes vs. the Beta reputation system shows the moderate superiority of the former model when it comes to utility and accuracy (for maximal selection), while for a probabilistic selection the Beta reputation system performs better with respect to accuracy, but not so well with respect to utility. These are just two examples—for a more extensive comparison of various trust and reputation models the reader is advised to look at [16].

In summary, in order to avoid ad hoc evaluations of computational trust and reputation management systems appropriate testing environments, called testbeds, are needed. A trust test-bed is an independent and easy-to-use platform for bench-marking trust models by evaluating them against a set of well-defined scenarios and metrics. This way the basic scientific premises can be adhered to by providing a controlled environment for experiments that can be measured, and repeatedly validated under the same conditions.

3.4 A Taxonomy for Trust and Reputation Management Systems

The concluding part of this chapter is an appropriate place to provide a taxonomy of trust and reputation management systems for two reasons. First, such a taxonomy is needed in the next chapter when it comes to the development and integration these systems for operational environments. In must be remarked that the lack of conceptual clarity may lead to implementation problems, thus hindering the implemented systems' interoperability, and so on. Second, taxonomies are key pillars for the derivation of ontologies, which are needed for semantic integration of data from various sources and their machine based interpretation. Trust and management related data do come from heterogeneous sources and will have a variety of native syntax representations and semantic properties.

Therefore our taxonomy of trust and reputation systems will be focused on implementation. In order to derive it an extensive review of these systems as given in [36] and [30] will serve as the starting point. These are one of the most extensive reviews in the literature, therefore they provide a good basis by considering all relevant elements in order to obtain a taxonomy that will be instructive enough, but not overloaded with too many details. Ideally, a taxonomy should be easy to comprehend, detailed to an appropriate level and not more than this.

The trust and reputation management systems review given in [36] is built upon different categories, which cover models of reference, information sources, visibility, behaviour assumptions, types of information exchanged and reliability:

1. The model of reference covers both a cognitive model and a game-theoretical model, which can be characterized as follows:

   - The cognitive model is based on the mental states of agents that drive the trust towards another agent or that assign its reputation.
   - The game-theoretical model is based on subjective probabilities calculated by an individual, therefore trust (or reputation) is not the result of a mental state, but of rational analysis judged along some utility function.

2. Information sources cover all possible channels that enable trust and reputation values to be obtained:

   - Direct experience, which is the most credible source (if communicated honestly). It can be based on direct interaction, or the (direct) observed interaction, of other agents within a community.
   - Indirect information is the second-hand information acquired as a result of witnessing, word of mouth, etc. This kind of information is more prone to manipulations and its credibility is often more questionable.
   - Sociological information, which is a kind of implicit information that is based on the roles that agents play in a society (e.g. the role of a judge should imply some trust in a judge as such).
   - Prejudice is another form of indirect information and often an important one (it is not necessarily that prejudice is always negative, although this connotation is most often the case).

3. Visibility involves how trust and reputation is shared among members of a community. It can be global or subjective (intimate).
4. Behaviour assumptions play a crucial role as trust and reputation values can be communicated correctly, or skewed—be it intentionally or unintentionally.
5. The nature of exchanged information is about the type of trust and reputation assessments—are they descriptive, given as probabilities, etc.?
6. Reliability is about providing additional attributes that further support the evaluation of trust and reputation values.

Considering the above categories and sub-categories that are focused on trust and reputation phenomena for artificial intelligence agents environments, their aggregation and general implementations focused structuring gives the taxonomy shown in Fig. 3.7. It starts with whether the system deals with rational or non-rational assessments (or both). It continues with the typifying of assessments: are these qualitative or quantitative (or are both areas supported)? Next, are only individual or also group assessments (or both) supported? Next, is the assessment direct or indirect? Furthermore, does the system support reliability (e.g. filters to focus on manipulators, liars, and also the possibility of self-assessment for the provided information)? Finally, is evidence, as well as context, supported?

Summing up, the above taxonomy provides sufficient, but not overly detailed implementation guidance.

*   *   *

There is another kind of systems that one would expect to fall within the scope of this chapter. These are recommender systems and they appear to have a lot to do with trust and reputation. But this is not the case, recommender systems are actually systems that try to match a user's preferences when it comes to products or services. On this basis they offer similar services that the user may be interested in buying, or consuming in some way (for more information on recommender systems the reader is referred to [33]).

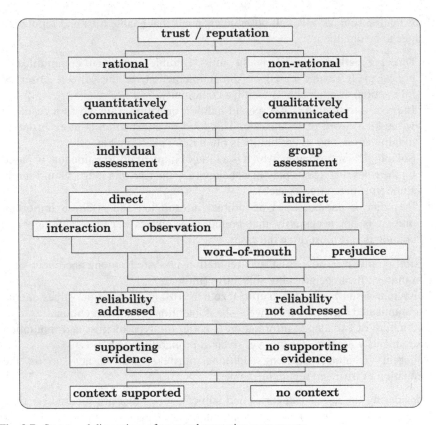

Fig. 3.7 Structured dimensions of trust and reputation assessments

References

1. A. Abdul-Rahman, S. Hailes, Supporting trust in virtual communities, in *Proceedings of the 33rd Hawaii International Conference on System Sciences-Volume 6 - Volume 6*, HICSS '00, Washington, DC (IEEE Computer Society, New York, 2000), p. 6007
2. M.S. Al-Mutairi, K.W. Hipel, M.S. Kamel, Trust and cooperation from a fuzzy perspective. Math. Comput. Simul. **76**(5–6), 430–446 (2008)
3. M.Y. Becker, A.R. Becker, N. Sultana, Foundations of logic-based trust management, in *IEEE Symposium on Security and Privacy, SP* 2012, 21–23 May 2012, San Francisco, California (2012), pp. 161–175
4. A.J. Bidgoly, B.T. Ladani, Benchmarking reputation systems. Comput. Hum. Behav. **57**(C), 274–291 (2016)
5. Cambridge University Press, *Cambridge Advanced Learner's Dictionary* (Cambridge University Press, Cambridge, 2008)
6. J. Carbo, J.M. Molina, J. Davila, Trust management through fuzzy reputation. Int. J. Cooperative Inf. Syst. **12**(01), 135–155 (2003)
7. C. Castelfranchi, R. Falcone, Principles of trust for MAS: cognitive anatomy, social importance, and quantification, in *ICMAS '98: Proceedings of the 3rd International Conference on Multi Agent Systems*, pp. 72–79, Washington, DC (IEEE Computer Society, New York, 1998)

8. Y. Cheng, *The Standard Model and Beyond* (Springer International Publishing, Cham, 2017), pp. 5–11
9. P. Cofta, *Trust, Complexity and Control: Confidence in a Convergent World.* (Wiley, Chichester, 2007)
10. D.E. Comer, *Internetworking with TCP/IP*, 6th edn. (Prentice-Hall, Inc., Upper Saddle River, NJ, 2013)
11. ConsumerReports, The truth about online ratings services - online ratings services promise unbiased reviews of local businesses. web resource. Last Accessed 4 Sept 2016
12. D.E. Denning, A new paradigm for trusted systems, in *Proceedings on the 1992–1993 Workshop on New Security Paradigms*, NSPW '92-93, New York, NY (ACM, New York, 1993), pp. 36–41
13. D. Gambetta, Can we trust trust? in *Trust: Making and Breaking Cooperative Relations* (Basil Blackwell, Oxford, 1988), pp. 213–237
14. Government Office for Science, Distributed ledger technology: beyond block chain. Technical Report 0, UK Government (2016)
15. T. Grandison, M. Sloman, A survey of trust in internet applications. Commun. Surv. Tutorials **3**(4), 2–16 (2000)
16. D. Jelenc, R. Hermoso, J. Sabater-Mir, D. Trcek, Decision making matters: a better way to evaluate trust models. Knowl.-Based Syst. **52**, 147–164 (2013)
17. A. Jøsang, Trust-based decision making for electronic transactions, in *Proceedings of the Fourth Nordic Workshop on Secure Computer Systems (NORDSEC'99* (1999)
18. A. Jøsang, *Subjective Logic: A Formalism for Reasoning Under Uncertainty* (Springer, Heidelberg, 2016)
19. A. Jøsang, R. Ismail, C. Boyd, A survey of trust and reputation systems for online service provision. Decis. Support Syst. **43**(2), 618–644 (2007)
20. E. Koutrouli, A. Tsalgatidou, Reputation systems evaluation survey. ACM Comput. Surv. **48**(3), 35:1–35:28 (2015)
21. S.P. Marsh, Formalising trust as a computational concept. PhD thesis, University of Stirling (1994)
22. D.H. McKnight, N.L. Chervany, The meanings of trust. Working Paper (1996)
23. Merriam-Webster Online, Merriam-Webster Online Dictionary. Merriam-Webster Publishing (2009)
24. D. Meunier, R. Lambiotte, E. Bullmore, Modular and hierarchically modular organization of brain networks. Front. Neurosci. **4**, 200 (2010)
25. L. Mui, Computational models of trust and reputation: agents, evolutionary games, and social networks. PhD thesis, MIT (2002)
26. L. Mui, A. Halberstadt, M. Mohtashemi, Ratings in distributed systems: a Bayesian approach, in *11th Workshop on Information Technologies and Systems (WITS)* (2001)
27. L. Ninghui, J.C. Mitchell, W.H. Winsborough, Design of a role-based trust-management framework, in *2002 IEEE Symposium on Security and Privacy, 2002. Proceedings* (2002), pp. 114–130
28. L. Page, S. Brin, R. Motwani, T. Winograd, The pagerank citation ranking: bringing order to the web. Technical Report 1999-66, Stanford InfoLab, November (1999). Previous number = SIDL-WP-1999-0120
29. A. Pimlott, O. Kiselyov, *Soutei, a Logic-Based Trust-Management System*, ed. by M. Hagiya, P. Wadler (Springer, Berlin, 2006), pp. 130–145
30. I. Pinyol, J. Sabater-Mir, Computational trust and reputation models for open multi-agent systems: a review. Artif. Intell. Rev. **40**(1), 1–25 (2013)
31. L. Rainie, B. Wellman, *Networked: The New Social Operating System* (MIT Press, Cambridge, 2012)
32. P. Resnick, K. Kuwabara, R. Zeckhauser, E. Friedman, Reputation systems. Commun. ACM **43**(12), 45–48 (2000)
33. F. Ricci, L. Rokach, B. Shapira, P.B. Kantor, *Recommender Systems Handbook*, 1st edn. (Springer, New York, 2010)

34. J. Sabater, C. Sierra, Regret: reputation in gregarious societies, in *Proceedings of the Fifth International Conference on Autonomous Agents*, AGENTS '01, New York, NY (ACM, New York, 2001), pp. 194–195
35. J. Sabater, C. Sierra, Social regret, a reputation model based on social relations. SIGecom Exch. **3**(1), 44–56 (2001)
36. J. Sabater, C. Sierra, Review on computational trust and reputation models. Artif. Intell. Rev. **24**(1), 33–60 (2005)
37. P. Samuelson, Altruism as a problem involving group versus individual selection in economics and biology. Am. Econ. Rev. **83**(2), 143–48 (1993)
38. D. Trcek, A. Brodnik, Hard and soft security provisioning for computationally weak pervasive computing systems in e-health. IEEE Wirel. Commun. **20**(4), 22–29 (2013)
39. D. Trček, *Managing Information Systems Security and Privacy* (Springer, Heidelberg, 2006)
40. D. Trček, An integrative architecture for a sensor-supported trust management system. Sensors **12**(8), 10774 (2012)
41. D. Trček, Computational trust management, QAD, and its applications. Informatica **25**(21), 139–154 (2014)
42. D. Trček, Qualitative assessment dynamics - complementing trust methods for decision making. Int. J. Inf. Technol. Decis. Mak. **13**(01), 155–173 (2014)
43. D. Trček, G. Kandus, Trust management in e-business systems - from taxonomy to trust engine architecture, in *WSEAS International Conference on System Science, Applied Mathematics & Computer Science and Power Engineering Systems* (2002), pp. 1891–1895
44. R.R. Yager, J. Kacprzyk, M. Fedrizzi, (eds.), *Advances in the Dempster-Shafer Theory of Evidence* (Wiley, New York, 1994)
45. E. Zupančič, D. Trček, Qade: a novel trust and reputation model for handling false trust values in e-commerce environments with subjectivity consideration. Technol. Econ. Dev. Econ. 1–30 (2015)

Chapter 4
An Implementation Roadmap

There is nothing better than a good reputation.
(Hebrew proverb)

Various kinds of trust and reputation systems will exist in the foreseeable future. On one hand, they will include traditional solutions, which have already been in place for a number of years, while, on the other hand, a variety of new methods and models is emerging. How to deal with this variety?

In the field of IT, more particularly computer communications, we have learned an important lesson. It does not really matter how a certain system is designed and implemented as long as this system's interconnection with other systems is enabled—because connectivity matters. The internal functioning of a system may remain hidden as long as a clear interface is defined at its outer border. This interface covers the exchanged data syntax, semantics, and the procedure for data exchange, i.e. the protocol. Following such elementary principles, the current internet has developed a plethora of services and has resulted in a complex structure that is among the most complex ones that humans have ever created. The lesson for trust and reputation management systems is therefore that appropriate interfaces and open protocols are needed to enable maximal integration.

When it comes to implementation of these systems, everything starts with organisation's business needs (see Fig. 4.1). In line with these needs, appropriate models have to be selected and evaluated to pinpoint the right ones. To make trust and reputation solution operable, this solution has to be protected accordingly. Next, feeding the core application with data can be started, where these data range from direct inputs from users to data from other sources on the web.

The following sections are written in such a way that they provide the big picture of the technological puzzle. Trust and reputation management technologies are still evolving and their ubiquitous deployment will be an issue for the foreseeable future. Therefore the steps provided in this chapter anticipate future developments in the area. They are aimed at providing a sufficiently detailed understanding of the necessary technologies and how these can be deployed in a particular organisation

© The Author(s) 2018
D. Trček, *Trust and Reputation Management Systems*,
SpringerBriefs in Information Systems, DOI 10.1007/978-3-319-62374-0_4

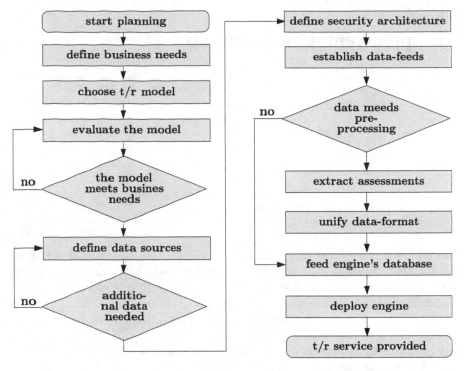

Fig. 4.1 Trust and reputation systems implementation planning (the "t" stands for trust, while "r" stands for reputation)

in a standardised way to ensure the interoperability and integration according to the current state of the art. Last but not least, the end of this chapter addresses important business issues.

4.1   Understanding the Necessary Information Technology Puzzle

Knowing that an interoperable and global network of trust and reputation management systems is our goal, there are quite a few technological building blocks that have to be put in place.

At the very core of such a structure are computer communications. The low level data transport and exchange support is a stable kind of infrastructure enabled by the TCP/IP communications stack (this subject is extensively addressed in many places in the literature, e.g. [28] or [11]). However, one particular part of the highest level of communications, i.e. the application layer of communication stack protocols, requires our closer involvement and understanding: web services.

From the architectural point of view, there are two basic kinds of web services (WS). The first one is the Representational State Transfer, or REST architecture [14], while the second one is the Simple Objects Access Protocol (or SOAP) architecture [15]. REST architecture[1] is about so called slim WS being tied to the basic web protocol, which is the Hypertext Transfer Protocol (or HTTP). On the other hand, SOAP is about the so called fat WS with more flexibility, and is not tied only to HTTP. Therefore REST architecture enables simple, but effective kinds of WS, while SOAP is more flexible, but there is a price to pay for its complexity ("Gone are the days when SOAP was simple." as cited in [30]).

In the majority of cases the above two families of WS provide a sufficient basis for businesses needs when it comes to data exchange between trust and reputation management systems. However, data exchange is just one component. Throughout this book we have analysed numerous trust and reputation management systems and models with various kinds of ratings and their semantics. Therefore, an effective, possibly machine supported interpretation and automated deployment of exchanged data is what is needed. If possible, hidden knowledge in the data about trust and reputation should be made explicit as well. And that is where semantic web technologies come into play.

Semantic web technologies are based on web and artificial intelligence methods. Using a semantic web is not the only possible approach to address our needs, but it has important advantages: these technologies are quite stable, related tools are available, and they are extensively standardised.[2] Nevertheless, connectivity for data exchange comes first.

4.1.1   Light Web Services: REST and RESTful Architectures

REST is an acronym for Representational State Transfer. This is a kind of architecture that is at the core of the web as we know it. It is about simple interactions between clients and servers often having the following form:

- Using his/her web browser, the user sends a request for a particular web page from a server.
- The server interprets the request and returns the wanted web page to the browser, which then properly formats it and displays it.

---

[1]An implementation that follows the REST architectural paradigm is referred to as a RESTful application.

[2]Ongoing activities in this regard are best followed at https://www.w3.org/2013/data/.

In many cases, however, this elementary kind of interaction is not sufficient, therefore REST architecture enables more complex interactions, such as the following [1]:

- Using his/her web browser, the user initiates the interaction and sends a request to a server to obtain a particular kind of feed-back information that is of a more complex nature.
- The server interprets the request, returns the appropriate response and eventually provides additional input fields to enable further processing of the user's request.
- The user fills in the missing data and sends them back.
- The server processes the received document with the user's data and decides if this is sufficient, or if additional pages have to be sent to the user to complete the current procedure. When there is nothing else needed for a particular process to be exchanged, the server sends the final, confirmation page to the user.

The REST architecture provides a common interface that is coupled with the Hypertext Transfer Protocol and where the following methods are offered:

- GET—this method is used to retrieve a representation of a resource;
- HEAD—this method is only used to retrieve the header of a response that would be provided by the GET method;
- POST—this method enables actions to be performed on the server side (e.g. creating new resources, modifying existing ones, etc.);
- PUT—this method completely updates or replaces an existing resource, or can create a completely new resource;
- DELETE—this method, as its name implies, deletes a resource;
- TRACE—this method triggers a server to reflect back the received header;
- OPTIONS—this method triggers a server to provide a description of supported services (possibilities).

The central concept of REST architecture is that it is about resources, where a resource has to be considered in the broadest terms. The only condition, however, is that it is identifiable. For this identification, the so called Uniform Resource Identifier (URI) is used, and it is standardised in [4].

The URI is a sequence of characters that uniquely identifies an abstract or physical resource, and is typically hierarchically structured. A URI is often used interchangeably with a universal resource locator (URL). But URLs are actually a subset of URIs that, in addition to identifying a resource, provide the means of accessing the resource. To further confuse the situation, the term uniform resource name (URN) has been introduced, and has been used historically to refer to both, URI and URL. So, a few examples of URIs according to the above standard are as follows:

```
http://www.ietf.org/rfc/rfc2396.txt,
ftp://ftp.is.co.za/rfc/rfc1808.txt,
urn:oasis:names:specification:docbook:dtd:xml:4.1.2.
```

The last example above is a self-expressive URI as it provides a hierarchically structured identification of a particular specification (document book). As to the means of accessing this resource, this kind of URI provides no hints. Contrary to the last URI, the first two URIs are URLs and URLs also provide the means of accessing a resource. In the first case the given URL specifies the Hyper-text Transfer Protocol (HTTP) for accessing the RFC 2396 document that resides on the WWW server in the domain ietf.org. In the second case, the protocol is the File Transfer Protocol (FTP), which enables access to RFC 1808 document on the FTP server in a domain is.co.za.

By deploying URIs, servers provide clients, i.e. users, with resources. More precisely, they provide users with a representation of a resource and these resources are referred to in a protocol between a client and a server. There may be various kinds of representations of the resources. Most often this is hypertext mark-up language (HTML) representation, or extended mark-up language (XML) representation. HTML is almost exclusively focused on how a certain resource (web page) is presented in a browser. XML has much broader functionality since it also provides processing instructions for other applications, like checking the proper structuring of a document, its transformations into other forms, and so on.

Suppose we are using a REST WS and we want to obtain information about the reputation of a user John in a certain society. The corresponding request and response are given below:

```
1# Request
2GET /user/john HTTP/1.1
3Host: www.reputations.org
```

```
1# Response
2HTTP/1.1 200 OK
3Content-Type: application/xml;charset=UTF-8
4
5<reputation>
6 <id> urn:exampleCommunity:user:john </id>
7 <value>high</value>
8</reputation>
```

The first line in the request states the method for obtaining data about the user John, while the second line shows the server name this request is being sent to. In response the first line states status (which is OK) and the second line states that the response contains an XML message. It also states how it is coded. After these two header lines the actual reputation value (which is high) is given and structured as an XML document.

XML is a superset of HTML and it is crucial for the majority of web related technologies. Trust and reputation management systems are no exception. Understanding XML is important for the implementation of trust and reputation management systems, which will have to be tightly coupled with the web.

XML is specified by the W3C Consortium [7]. It is a tagged language where its elements have names (denoted by tags) and values (these are given between tags). So, for example, in the simple structure below the tags <myElement> and </myElement> denote an element, which has a value "This is my element":

```
<myElement>
 This is my element
</myElement>
```

Using tags, various elements can be put together to form rich structures that comprise XML documents (as mentioned, these documents are not just about data presentation, but also about processing instructions). The structure of XML documents is not just any kind of structure. Here are the most important requirements for XML documents:

- XML documents have to be well-formed, meaning that the elements have to be hierarchically structured (one element is at the top level, followed by one or more elements at the next level, and so on until the lowest level). This structure prohibits one element at the same hierarchical level from being interleaved with another element.[3] As to the characters that are allowed in elements' names (tags' characters), these must start with a character or an underscore, may not contain blanks (space characters), may contain letters, digits, hyphens, underscores, periods, colons, full-stops, and they are case sensitive. For elements values it is a wise practice to follow the allowed characters for element's names with the addition of spaces, as well as single and double quotation marks.
- XML documents may have to be valid. This requirement further narrows the set of acceptable documents among well-formed ones to those that are acceptable for a particular purpose and processing. The validity of an XML document is in principle optional, but in reality an XML document is almost always associated with a so called XML schema. This schema serves as a kind of a template that a particular XML document has to structurally adhere to [5, 13, 29] (a more detailed description of their use can be found in [31]). When the document adheres to this schema it is said to be valid.

In brief, well-formedness is simply a core requirement that is needed to produce an XML document, which meets the very basic requirements for general processing. The validity further narrows the set of acceptable documents to those that are aligned with a particular kind of processing, like those required by a concrete application. Valid documents are obtained by deploying XML a schemas. To state only the most important properties of a schema: a schema specifies what elements a document should have, what the sequence of these elements should be, how many repetitions of these elements are allowed, and what types of elements are allowed (of course, the schema document itself is an XML document).

---

[3] As nicely put in [6], one should think of an XML document as a linearization of a tree structure. At every node in the tree there are several character strings. The tree structure and the character strings together form the information content of an XML document.

Suppose now we have a person (a subject) called Tom and a digital object, which is a song performed by Tom, in MP3 format, accessible at URL

`http://www.songs.org/toms_Song.mp3`.

So Tom (a subject) is performing (this is a predicate) a song called Tom's Song (an object). This fact can be represented as in the following XML document:

```
1<?xml version="1.0" encoding="UTF-8"?>
2<triplet xmlns:xsi="http://www.w3.org/2001/XMLSchema-instance"
3  xsi:noNamespaceSchemaLocation="semanticData.xsd">
4  <subject>
5   Tom
6  </subject>
7  <predicate>
8   isPerforming
9  </predicate>
10 <object>
11  Tom's Song
12 </object>
13</triplet>
```

The above triplet, subject—predicate—object (also referred to as subject—property—object triplet), is at the core of semantic web technologies, which are addressed in the next subsection. The whole file above is rather self-descriptive. The first line is declaring that this is an XML file and that its coding is UTF-8. The second and the third line serve to define a so called name space. The name space ensures that the tags used are unique, so even if some other application uses the same tags everything is fine as long as they belong to some other name space. Further, the third line specifies the XSD file with schema that is used to validate this particular document. This the schema is given below:

```
1 <xs:schema xmlns:xs="http://www.w3.org/2001/XMLSchema">
2  <xs:element name="semanticTriplet">
3   <xs:complexType>
4    <xs:sequence>
5     <xs:element type="xs:string" name="subject"/>
6     <xs:element type="xs:string" name="predicate"/>
7     <xs:element type="xs:string" name="object"/>
8    </xs:sequence>
9   </xs:complexType>
10  </xs:element>
11</xs:schema>
```

As was the case with the first XML document, the above schema is rather self-descriptive. The first line again provides its name space, followed by the definition of a semantic triplet, which is a sequence of three elements with the names subject, predicate and object.

4.1.2 Complex Web Services: SOAP Based Architectures

SOAP based architectures are a well established and widespread kind of technology that has been around for many years. These kind of services complement REST services, as SOAP based architectures are able to support complex transactions by chaining various services and controlling them in a programmatic way. So each of these services may perform a certain operation, while the whole chain of these operations performs a complex service that may reassemble a complete business process such as automated software sales.

The core concept of SOAP architectures is that various services will reside on the Internet and they will be provided by different vendors. To be able to deploy them they have to be described accordingly. For this purpose Web Services Description Language (WSDL) is used. WSDL describes an interface to a service concerning where on the Internet it resides, how to access it (what data in what format to submit to), and what is provided by the service. Based on the WSDL description, one forms a SOAP message and sends a SOAP request to the service. After receiving this request the WS performs intended operation, and, when required so, provides a SOAP response.

The SOAP message consists of an envelope and attachments (it is standardized in [32]). The envelope is mandatory and it contains a header with zero or more entries, and a body which is also mandatory, while the header and the attachments are optional. SOAP uses request and response messages. To illustrate its use, suppose we are deploying SOAP to obtain the relative uptime of a sensor located in hall A, which is used to calculate the trust value assigned by some user to this sensor. With the following message we request the uptime value for the observed sensor:

```
1  <?xml version="1.0" encoding="UTF-8"?>
2  <soap-env:Envelope
3   xmlns:soap-env="http://schemas.xmlsoap.org/soap/envelope/"
4   xmlns:xsd="http://www.w3.org/2001/XMLSchema">
5    <soap-env:Header/>
6    <soap-env:Body>
7     <tns:getLocalSensorUptime
8       xmlns:tns="urn:UptimeMeasurement"
9       soap-env:encodingStyle=
10      "http://schemas.xmlsoap.org/soap/encoding/">
11      <hall xmlns:xsi="http://www.w3.org/2001/XMLSchema-instance"
12      xsi:type="xsd:string"> Hall A </hall>
12    </tns:getLocalSensorUptime>
14   </soap-env:Body>
15</soap-env:Envelope>
```

Upon obtaining this request, the SOAP based WS forms a response with the desired uptime value:

```
1  <?xml version="1.0" encoding="UTF-8"?>
2  <soap-env:Envelope
3    xmlns:soap-env="http://schemas.xmlsoap.org/soap/envelope/"
4    xmlns:xsi="http://www.w3.org/2001/XMLSchema-instance"
```

```
 5   xmlns:xsd="http://www.w3.org/2001/XMLSchema">
 6   <soap-env:Body>
 7   <ns1:getLocalSensorUptimeResponse
 8    xmlns:ns1="urn:UptimeMeasurement"
 9    soap-env:encodingStyle=
10    "http://schemas.xmlsoap.org/soap/encoding/">
11    <return xsi:type="xsd:decimal"> 0.977 </return>
12   </ns1:getLocalSensorUptimeResponse>
13</soap-env:Body>
14</soap-env:Envelope>
```

Although the messages are again rather self-descriptive, a more detailed explanation follows. The first line of both messages is an XML file declaration. In both messages, the envelope element follows next with attributes that define name-spaces and aliases for easier referencing of the defined name-spaces (an example of a name-space in the first message is http://schemas.xmlsoap.org/soap/envelope/, which is the name-space for the SOAP envelope, and its elements are specified by prepending them with alias `soap-env`). The required method, which is called (`getLocalSensorUptime`) and sensor location (`Hall A`) are given in the body part of the first message. The body of the second message analogously contains the method called `getLocalSensorUptimeResponse` and the reported uptime value `0.977`.

What remains is to provide the WSDL description of the service (the latest version of WSDL language is standardised in [10]). The WSDL description file defines API provided calls, objects and fields, which are available to the outer world by this particular WS (in cases when WS is hosted in a cloud, the cloud provider may generate the required WSDL file). So the whole SOAP based service deployment scenario looks as given in Fig. 4.2.

In summary, while REST architecture is tied to HTTP protocol, SOAP based WS are transport protocol independent as well as being extensible and rather easily deployable in a distributed way. REST solutions are, on the other hand, easy to learn and deploy, require minimal processing, and can use more compact data

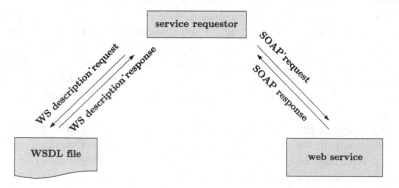

Fig. 4.2 SOAP web services architecture

representations, but they assume a direct, point-to-point communication. This nicely describes the complementarity between SOAP and REST architectures.

4.1.3   Semantic Web and Complementary Technologies

Getting trust and reputation values from one engine database into another engine database is one thing, but appropriate mapping between the values is another thing, because in many cases one format and semantics will differ from another. Suppose a source trust engine uses Marsh' formalism, while a target one uses eBay assessments, then appropriate mapping certainly becomes an issue. Furthermore, a lot of trust and reputation related information is not in an explicit form. They may be implicitly contained in an organisation's documents, various e-mails, spread over the web, and so on. Automatic derivation of values in such cases is still a bit of a dream, but with some involvement of human experts usable results can be obtained even today.

To successfully deal with this situation, semantic technologies offer one promising approach as do data mining technologies, especially those that focus on mining of text documents. These two will be covered next.

Semantic web technologies have been around for quite a few years now. Their basis is the XML language, which has been upgraded into more complex structures that form the core of the semantic web. So, these are the main building blocks and have the following corresponding specifications:

- Resource description framework, or RDF [17];
- Resource description framework schema, or RDFS [8];
- Web ontology language, or OWL [24].

RDF is at the heart of semantic web. It is a language that enables us to model the physical world, or any abstract world for that matter. The basic concept of RDF is a triplet subject—predicate—object (also referred to as object—property—subject, or resource—property—value), and some examples are shown in Fig. 4.3.

RDF is conceptualised around resources. Everything is a resource, including, of course, the elements of RDF triplets. Each resource of an RDF triplet can be a physical object, an abstract object, or a term. It is possible to link physical objects (things) to physical objects, physical objects to concepts, concepts to physical objects, and concepts to concepts. A caveat: what is important with RDF is that these resources can only be identified by XML and they have to be uniquely identified using URIs.

Having a look at Fig. 4.3 it can be seen how an abstract triplet is transformed into an RDF triplet, which says that Einstein is the discoverer of the Theory of Relativity. What may be interesting is that the physical, real-world entity (Einstein in our case) has to be modelled using a URI. Such a situation seems a bit odd—the link to some web information about Einstein, despite pointing to an authoritative source, is not the same as Einstein himself. But this is an inherent peculiarity of RDF

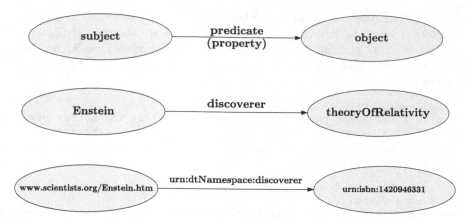

Fig. 4.3 The RDF model and some examples

conceptualisation. To provide another example for this peculiarity, let us consider a sports car that can accelerate from 0 to 100 km/h in 5 s, which means that it is capable of an acceleration of 5.6 m/(s*s):

```
1<?xml version="1.0"?>
2<rdf:RDF xmlns:rdf="http://www.w3.org/1999/02/22-rdf-syntax-ns#"
3         xmlns="http://www.vehicles.net/Cars#">
4 <SportsCar rdf:ID="Ferrari">
5    <acceleration>5.6 </acceleration>
6 </SportsCar>
7</rdf:RDF>
```

So our intention is to enrich the data about the sports car by its performance, more precisely its acceleration, and for this purpose we are using RDF. What is interesting to note is that the subject is the Ferrari car, the property (the predicate) is (about) acceleration, while the object is the actual acceleration performance of this Ferrari car—5.6 m/(s*s). This example demonstrates that the RDF concept of a resource should be considered broadly.

Now a more detailed description of the above structure follows. The first line is the XML file declaration line. The second line states that this is an RDF structure, and two name-spaces are provided: the one belonging to W3C and the other one belonging to www.vehicles.net. In the fourth line our subject is defined, followed by the predicate acceleration and the object, which is the actual acceleration that this Ferrari can achieve. The remaining two lines contain only closing tags as required for a well-formed XML document.

Instead of dealing directly with RDF, many operations can be carried out more easily by using the RDF Schema, or RDFS for short. RDF Schema is not radically different from RDF. It is intended to ease our work by providing core classes (like class rdfs:Resource or class rdfs:Property), core properties (like rdfs:subClasOf, rdfs:subPropertyOf), and core constraints (like rdfs:range, rdfs:doamin) [33].

Suppose we plan to add various attributes and relationships to cars in general, therefore it would be convenient to introduce class Car, where SportsCar is a subclass of class Car. Suppose further that we want to introduce class Racers that has members who possess sports cars. These facts can be represented with RDFS as follows:

```
1<?xml version="1.0"?>
2<rdf:RDF xmlns:rdf="http://www.w3.org/1999/02/22-rdf-syntax-ns#"
3          xmlns:rdfs="http://www.w3.org/2000/01/rdf-schema#"
4          xml:base="http://www.vehicles.net/Car.rdfs">
5    <rdfs:Class rdf:ID="Car">
6    </rdfs:Class>
7    <rdfs:Class rdf:ID="Driver">
8    </rdfs:Class>
9    <rdfs:Class rdf:ID="RacingCar">
10       <rdfs:subClassOf rdf:resource="#Car"/>
11   </rdfs:Class>
12   <rdfs:Class rdf:ID="Racer">
13       <rdfs:subClassOf rdf:resource="#Driver"/>
14   </rdfs:Class>
15   <rdf:Property rdf:ID="driven_by">
16       <rdfs:domain rdf:resource="#RacingCar"/>
17       <rdfs:range  rdf:resource="#Racer"/>
18   </rdf:Property>
19 </rdf:RDF>
```

The first line above declares that this is an XML file. The next three lines are needed for namespaces, where line 4 defines the namespace for car vocabulary. Next come classes Car, Driver, RacingCar and Racer, where the last two classes are subclasses of the first two (see lines 5 to 14). From lines 15 to 18 we define the property stating that racing cars are driven by racers. The last line concludes the schema.

The last step in semantic web standardisation is Web Ontology Language or OWL (not WOL as one would expect the acronym to be). It is another effort to further ease semantic expressions by adding new constructs. Compared to RDFS it is more complex and richer relationships can be expressed that greatly enhance reasoning ability (e.g. cardinality restrictions can be put in place, new classes by intersections of existing classes can be specified, etc.). Although such enhancements may seem rather trivial at first glance, this is not the case: they notably improve the strength of the apparatus.

The final goal of all these efforts is data interoperability that would enable reasoning about this data, which should be as automated as possible. In order to enable such efforts another kind of structure is needed. These are ontologies, and more specific motivations for their introduction are the following ones [33]:

- Ontologies enable a common understanding of key concepts in a certain domain, as they, by definition, entail the means for conceptualization of the observed domain.
- They make domain assumptions explicit.

- They provide ways of reusing existing knowledge.
- They enable knowledge (semantics) to be encoded in a machine-usable way. Consequently, large-scale (machine) processing is made possible that often leads to new knowledge, which is not obtainable on a small scale.

Ontologies certainly enable us to use existing knowledge about trust and reputation, to integrate related data, and to reason about trust and reputation. So the first attempts to come up with ontologies in our domain were carried out more than 10 years ago [9], while more recent efforts can be found in [2].

How can a high quality ontology be created? As mentioned, an ontology is a conceptualisation of the problem domain and it represents an organised body of knowledge (when the ontology concepts and their relationships are graphically represented, one obtains graphs with nodes and vertices). In order to obtain this organised body of knowledge the following, iterative procedure has to be applied [22]:

- First, one should determine the domain and the scope of the ontology. It should be made clear what the domain being covered is, what the purpose of ontology is, and what kind of answers the ontology should provide.
- Second, one should consider existing ontologies in the covered domain. Dictionaries, thesauruses and encyclopedias can serve as a starting point [20]. Dictionaries define terms, while thesauruses provide a network of related meanings. Encyclopedias, however, serve to extensively describe a concept once one knows what a concept is. Of course, existing ontologies can be (and should be) used in this step. They can be imported and afterwards extended or narrowed for a particular purpose.
- Third, one starts the enumeration process to itemize important terms in the ontology—what are the terms that ontology will be about, and what properties do these terms have. These terms are about concepts that are also referred to as classes, each of them having certain properties (attributes), and restrictions on these properties.
- Fourth, a classes hierarchy process has to be performed. This hierarchy may be obtained in a top-down manner, where the most general concept is taken first and narrowed down in further steps where sub-classes are introduced. It may also be obtained with a bottom-up approach where the most specific classes are defined first and then aggregated, step by step, into higher, more general concepts. It is also possible to follow the mixed approach and combine a top-down with bottom-up approach.
- Fifth, classes properties are defined (this process is also referred to as slots definition). This step is needed to describe the internal structure of concepts, i.e. classes, where these classes contain objects that may be physical or logical. The properties may be intrinsic, extrinsic, or may be a relationship. When classes are assigned properties, these properties are automatically assigned to subclasses, which is also referred to as inheritance.
- Sixth, the definition of properties is performed. In this step the type of property is defined (whether it is an integer, or an alphanumeric sequence, etc.), its

cardinality is defined (i.e. how many values a property may have), and what its domain and its range are (in this case the domain means the classes to which a slot is attached, while the allowed classes for a slot are its range).

- Seventh, instances have to be created. In order to define an individual instance of a class one has to choose the class, create an individual instance from it, and fill the slot values. For example, if a class charity organisation is chosen, we can create an individual instance Red Cross, where this instance has slots that may be defined as follows: name=RedCross, founder=Dunant&Moynier, type=non-profit, volunteers=13million, areaServed=worldwide, etc.

Developing an ontology is a rather tedious task and automated support is high on everyone's wish list. So it should come as no surprise that quite a number of such tools exist. Among them one reference implementation is Protege, developed at Stanford University.[4]

The main way of providing trust and reputation management engines with the needed assessments will be direct users' inputs. But mappings from one kind of trust and reputation format to another (as being required by another engine) will also be important. And this is where ontologies will come in handy. Experiences in other domains teach us that there will be various ontologies in the trust and reputation management domain, so their reuse will require some intermediate steps, referred to as ontology matching. Ontology matching has been extensively researched in other domains for years, therefore software tools exist that support users in this process (or partially automate it). However, ontology matching is an area of its own, so for a detailed and comprehensive description of approaches to ontology matching the reader is advised to look at [12].[5]

4.1.4   Extracting Content from General Data

Data lies around in various forms and formats, therefore trust and reputation related information is hidden in a great variety of sources. The problem now is how to extract the relevant content, interpret it accordingly, or how to explicitly enrich it with appropriate semantics to be usable for trust and reputation management systems, and if possible, to do this in as automated a way as possible. These goals are schematically presented in Fig. 4.4.

There are quite a few tools that offer support in the above goals, and among the reference tools is a software environment for statistical computing and graphics

---

[4]This software package is freely available at http://protege.stanford.edu/.

[5]A lot of work is going on in the research community and industry in this area. The literature, existing solutions and other details can be found at http://ontologymatching.org.

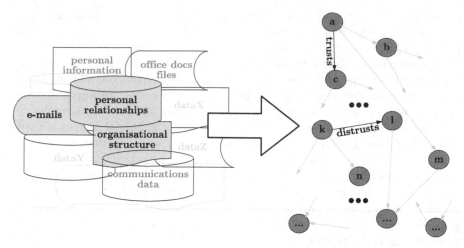

Fig. 4.4 Extracting trust and reputation related information from various data sources

called R.[6] This environment ranks among top tools for analytics and data mining, and although the following description relies on using R for these purposes, the steps are rather general when mining texts [34].

The procedure for mining texts consists of three main steps: First, the text has to be extracted from relevant sources like e-mails, web pages, tweets, etc. Second, the texts need to be transformed into a document-term matrix so that frequent words and associations can be searched for in this matrix. Third, important words are selected (like trust in our case) and this serves as a basis for performing an analysis on the included texts. Let's elaborate this in more detail.

The starting step, text extraction, depends on the source of the text. It can be done manually, but such a tedious task is now frequently supported by appropriate libraries or applications. Having the necessary texts in the corresponding documents, the so called corpus is obtained (corpus denotes a collection of relevant documents). In order to further streamline (or enable at all) the analysis, additional steps are performed. These include operations like converting upper case letters to lower case letters, removing punctuations, removing URLs, and so on. Afterwards, stemming has to be performed, which is needed to obtain words' radicals (e.g. the radical of trusted, trusts, trusting,... is trust). With this step all forms of the radical trust are prepared in order to determine their frequency. Now the term-document matrix can be derived (or its transposed matrix called the document-term matrix). In this matrix, the relationships between terms and corresponding documents are given. Rows stand for terms and columns for documents, so an entry in the matrix

---

[6]The R environment is available freely at https://www.r-project.org/. It has large community support and has been deployed in various domains with numerous successful applications, be it in academia or industry.

tells us the number of occurrences of a term in a particular document (while building this matrix terms with an insufficient frequency may be discarded). This is where the text preprocessing ends and the text mining can really start.

Now the analysis can be performed by, for example, checking the relevancy of our documents for trust. If trust and related terms like reputation, reliability and so on are among the most frequently used terms, this is fine. However, if none of these words appears among the top-ranking terms, then we should probably continue with our corpus building by looking for other additional sources of trust related data. Thus, if the frequency test passes a given threshold, then mining can continue. By using appropriate functions we can find associations between the term trust and terms that correlate with it by exceeding a certain correlation threshold (e.g. 0.5). This may give an analyst a hint as to how to derive certain trust and reputation assessment, or provide additional evidence to existing ones. In order to further support this process, various visualisations can be helpful; histograms are typically used in this process.

Deeper insight into texts may be provided by more advanced techniques like clustering. Using clustering, terms are grouped according to certain criteria. The data for this criteria are those contained in the term-document matrix (or document-term matrix). Using this data the distance between terms can be calculated and those that are closer form one cluster, another group of close-lying terms form another one, and so on. At different distances different clusters are identified, and these may be further structured into a so called dendrogram to present the hierarchy of clusters' structuring. But this is not the only possible approach, there are numerous available methods for clustering and more details can be found in, for example, [27].

4.1.5   Trust and Reputation Engine Infrastructure

Trust and reputation systems are built around so called engines. These engines are software systems that are fed by trust and reputation assessments (values), they perform the necessary calculations in line with the selected model, and provide outputs to users, which may be humans, or other e-services.

The core operations of trust and reputation engines are rather straightforward from the programming and implementation point of view. They perform mathematical (symbolic) operations defined by selected trust or reputation model, and these models, as presented in Chap. 3, often don't require sophisticated operations. The majority of implementation efforts therefore go elsewhere. It starts with obtaining and pre-processing the large amounts of dispersed, distributed data needed, while at the same time meeting the following requirements [27]:

- Trust and reputation systems should be designed for long-term accurate performance so that their scores can be taken with confidence. A natural consequence is that the system, for example, has to be able to distinguish between newcomers with unknown behaviour on one side, and an entity with long-term poor behaviour on the other.

- These systems should have a tendency to put higher weights on recent behaviour, and recent trends related to this behaviour. Clearly, one entity may decide to become better and has to be stimulated to do so, while someone who has decided (or being forced) to behave oddly despite good past performance, has to be identified as well.
- These systems should not be over-sensitive to a few fluctuations in opinions, e.g. outliers. Their operations should provide steady and smooth outputs. So, for example, a mistake or an exaggeration in an input opinion should not radically change the status of the observed entity.
- The engines should be resistant to traditional, security related attacks and hard security measures provide answers in this case. There will always be successful attacks, but the emerging paradigm in e-services is that when this happens, a system has to be returned to its normal operation as soon as possible. Preferably, without manual intervention.

These systems should be also resilient to attacks to assessments as these assessments are about core operations of trust and management systems. Preventing such attacks is probably the most difficult of all the issues, and it will be covered next.

4.1.6 Attacks on Core Functionality and Countermeasures

As opposed to traditional hard security measures that mostly involve cryptographic mechanisms and protocols, attacks aimed at subverting trust and management assessments and operators are quite different and more subtle. While the former kind of protection, which is used generally for protecting IT systems, is extensively covered in many places in the literature (see, for example, [30] or [3]), the latter kind of attacks remain almost unaddressed.

To provide intended core functionality, the first step is to ensure that an assessment is obtained at all. So, the first research studies focused on incentives to provide appropriate feed-back. One key observation found by Resnick et al. was that there was a notable disproportion between positive and negative feed-backs, with positive ones dominating strongly [23]. This study also exposed the problem of the generally low rate of feed-back, which moderately exceeded 50% (buyers provided feedback in 51.7% of cases, while sellers on buyers provided feed-back in 60.7% of cases). Authors saw the low-rate response as a kind of a free-rider problem, because those that do not make the least effort to provide feed-back are taking advantage of those that do.

Despite the above mentioned research, nothing has changed significantly and the low response rate and biased responses still remained an issue. To further complicate matters, other kinds of attacks have became increasingly common. In e-environments, where changing an identity requires minimal effort, users have started to take many fake identities and they use these to subvert the whole logic of trust and reputation management systems. Therefore, Resnick et al. have proposed increasing the economic cost of getting a new identity, which would raise the bar for those who want to misbehave.

Later research has resulted in a more refined classification of patterns of mis-behaviour, and has increased focus on specific, refined attacks, and counter-measures for preventing them [19, 21, 26]:

- The first kind of attack is when an adversary enters a system, and later leaves it to re-enter it under a different identity. This kind of attack is known as a white-washing (or re-entry or newcomer) attack and it enables an adversary to avoid the consequences of bad behaviour. A sub-variant is a traitor attack where an adversary starts out with good behaviour in order to gain a good reputation so that he or she behave badly when the chance arises.
- The second kind of attack is when an adversary intentionally provides false or unfair ratings, which is referred to as corruption or unfair ratings attack. An extension of this approach is alternating-behaviour attack: at certain times an attacker is a good citizen, but he or she otherwise misbehaves. An extension of this attack is discrimination attack, where an adversary has two types of behaviours: the adversary contributes high quality contributions to one system, and low quality ones to another. Another variant is ballot stuffing attack where an adversary assigns a positive feedback to a badly behaving agent. This attack is also known as false praise attack.
- The third kind of attack is a more complex one: a collusion attack. This occurs when malicious agents act in orchestration to cause more damage than when acting independently. If the majority of participants do this, the system becomes useless. In one variant, oscillation attack, malicious user identities are divided into different groups, where each group plays dynamically different roles. Some groups focus on improving their reputation feedback by providing honest feed-backs on unimportant objects, while other groups provide dishonest feedbacks. After a certain time the roles are dynamically switched. Another variant of the collusion attack is the raptrap attack. In this case malicious identities break the majority rule in coordination by subverting the honest feedback into a dishonest one. If a majority opinion is considered to be a key property of an assessment, this attack not only subverts real reputation, but also increases the feedback ratings of the malicious identities.
- The fourth kind of attack can be seen as an individualised version of a collusion attack: the Sybil attack. With this attack an attacker uses many identities simultaneously. By being able to provide numerous (faked) feed-back inputs into the system this attacker can seriously impact the results of the system, or completely subvert it.
- Finally, there is a reputation lag exploitation attack. This is an attack, where a participant initially provides correct inputs to obtain a good reputation. After the good reputation point is reached, a serious miss-information is submitted and due to the reputation level it is considered as to be very relevant.

The question is how one can counter the above described attacks. The research in this field is not very extensive, but certain promising approaches can be found in the literature [26]:

- To counter white-washing attack a restricted number of pseudonyms is proposed. This can be done on the basis of, for example, monitoring IP addresses of registering entities, or by introducing fees. Furthermore, newcomers can be assigned initially low reputation values in order to stimulate good behaviour. So called forgetting schemes may be implemented to prevent traitor attacks, in particular. Unfortunately, they also affect well-behaved agents. A more natural approach can be used where a gradual diminishing of reputation values as a function of time is implemented, which is referred to as adaptive forgetting.
- Dishonest feedbacks can be prevented by increasing their cost through the introduction of appropriate credentials like a record of real transactions. Dishonest feedbacks can be further prevented by studying the statistical features of feedbacks, e.g. a strong deviation from the majority of feed-backs may be a warning. Similarly, a feed-back that significantly increases the uncertainty of the feedback distribution may also be suspicious and could raise an alarm. Mitigating the effects of dishonest feedbacks can be supported by imposing schemes where the feed-back of users with low feedback reputation will have a lower impact on a particular reputation score.
- To prevent collusion attacks a temporal analysis has been proposed. This analysis tracks the times a feedback is provided, as well as the trends in its value changes. Another option is to deploy user correlation analysis, where the orchestrated activities outcomes serve to uncover the coordinated identities.

In the last case above it is shown that statistics based techniques may play an important role in preventing the attacks. Any rating can be considered as a kind of signal and its dynamics can be subject to signal processing techniques. In [26] some possible analyses of the time domain are given:

- To detect increases in rating activity, the arrival rate detector can be deployed. The incoming ratings are treated as a signal R, which is the number of daily ratings. Next we form a sliding window with $2W$ data from R. The first half of data in the window is denoted as X_1, and the second half as X_2. A reasonable assumption is that both halves follow a Poison distribution with arrival rate parameters λ_1 and λ_2. Now an algorithm is deployed to detect if there is a notable arrival rate change at the center of the window, i.e. $\lambda_1 \neq \lambda_2$. The arrival rate change curve is plotted next using the detection function for each of the sliding windows vs. the center time of the window. When an attack occurs between times t_1 and t_2 the detection curve may result in two peaks at t_1 and t_2.
- A variation of the above procedure is the mean change detector that detects sudden changes of the mean of rating values. In this case the attacker is detected that wants to boost or reduce the aggregated reputation score. A histogram observation algorithm can also be used to detect such subverting efforts.

- Another option for detecting colluded users is to let $x(n)$ denote the n rating values, therefore $E(x(n))$ gives the mean value of this sequence of values. In the case of no collusion attacks the difference $x(n) - E(x(n))$ is expected to exhibit white noise properties, while deviation from such a situation is a signal that needs addressing. More precisely, an autoregressive signal model is used and its error is examined. When this error is high, white noise is being observed. When it is low there is higher probability that $x(n)$ contains a signal that is the result of colluding users.

These approaches based on temporal analysis provide certain counter-measures to attacks. In order to improve their efficiency, they may be combined one with another to uncover those time intervals that are suspicious. This may lead to the automatic removal of suspicious ratings, which can be further improved by user correlation analysis [18]. In this latter case suspicious users in suspicious intervals are searched for. Ratings of suspicious users X and Y are collected (both those that are honest and those that represent attacks) and if there are n rated objects by X and Y, then these ratings are denoted as $\{x_1, x_2, \ldots, x_n\}$ and $\{y_1, y_2, \ldots, y_n\}$, respectively. The Euclidean distance between X and Y can be then be obtained:

$$d(X, Y) = \sqrt{\sum_{i=1}^{n}(x_i - y_i)^2} \tag{4.1}$$

This distance is calculated for each pair taken from the set of suspicious users and then clustered according to this distance (the more suspicious the users, the smaller the distance). For each cluster the group rating is calculated that is the average rating score of users in this particular cluster related to an attacked object. During an attack the cluster with the highest group rating is the one most suspicious.

While the above approaches protect against subversion attacks, they also have limitations. First, an aggregated boosting may be the result of a real change in the behaviour of an observed entity. Second, the use of common distributions for trust and reputation management system may be based on rather broad assumptions. For example, consider feedbacks that we know are inherently reported in a biased way, where there is a higher proportion of feed-back related to positive encounters than negative ones. A similar reasoning applies to assumptions with regard to traffic patterns.

4.2 Wrapping It All Up

So far we have provided the necessary technological building blocks belonging to a de facto (and de iure) standards-compliant arsenal of solutions needed for establishing trust and reputation systems (see the Fig. 4.5). The next steps are about implementing these building blocks within a particular organisation's information

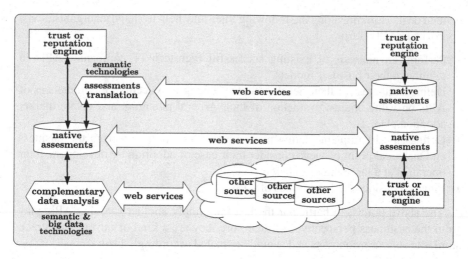

Fig. 4.5 Integration of all components in the trust and reputation management systems domain

system by following established methodologies for information systems development and implementation (one such recent and frequently used approach is the Scrum method [25]).

However, this section has a different twist and provides a perspective that may appear rather surprising at first glance. The focus here is on application program interfaces, or APIs. Although APIs are about pure technology, their far-more wide-reaching role is as a gateway to e-business strategies and operations. Considering the almost unimaginable success of companies like Google, Facebook, Twitter, and Netflix (to name only a few) the central question is "What is the key factor behind their success?" And more often than not the answer is: their business models. Knowing that these are high-tech IT companies and going deeper into the details behind their business models, the key common elements that surface are Application Program Interfaces.

And just what are APIs? What do they provide? As nicely put in [16], APIs provide support to other developers and businesses in developing their services to access your services and data.

APIs often seem to be a rather trivial issue to programmers and techies. However, their impact on business can not be overstated. They affect integration with other service providers, enable services extensibility and have strong business transformation potential. In some cases they even contribute to the creation of new industries. So from a business point of view APIs are an important and complex issue and for successful trust and reputation management systems implementation this topic must be addressed.

When an organisation considers the definition of its API, things have to be well-thought out, because the whole business model of a particular company may depend on it. Thinking along the following lines may help to shape an organisation's approach to APIs [16]:

- Perform an analysis of existing successful high-tech IT companies APIs in relation to their business models.
- Define strategies for their development by taking into account the influences of APIs on value chains, evaluation of their general potential, and create market adoption plan.
- Define an API implementation plan, metrics for evaluation from the business and technical point of view, consider their ease of adoption by developers, their operation at a large scale, and their security.
- Finally, consider the legal issues of APIs.

The above points, in particular the last one, imply another role that APIs play from the bushiness perspective. At their core they are a kind of informal contract, similar to software contracts and should be treated accordingly [16]:

- The API provider should describe what functionality is offered from the high-level business perspective. This includes details as to what functionality will be available in the future, how compatibility will be addressed, and how eventual incompatible changes in an API will be handled.
- The API provider has to give the technological details that are needed by applications and services developers to integrate their services and applications with the API. These details are not just about technological (programming level) details like access protocol specifications, but also about the limits on the number of users, the hours and days of no availability, maintenance outages, etc.
- An API has to be bound by a consent from developers' side as to the terms of use of the API, adherence to the provider's requirements, and other necessary legal issues.

For a better representation and understanding of the interplay between APIs, early business models and their evolutionary dynamics the scheme in Fig. 4.6 is given [16]. Related business models can be roughly divided into free and non-free models. Free models are intentionally split into those that are unconditionally free to distinguish them from those that are free only if certain restrictions are met. An example of this would be to develop an application based on an API that is free, but where the use of this API requires that your application is also provided for free.

As to non-free models, these can be divided into direct and indirect ones. Direct models roughly comprise those where a developer gets paid, and those where a developer pays for using an API:

- When a developer has to pay, one option is the tiered model with different levels of usage. Straightforward variants are the pre-payment models (also called pay as you go models) and the unit-based model (where a unit may consist of a basic subscription plus some quanta based on the API's usage, or may be a transaction as such). The freemium model is the model where the API itself is not charged for, but additional services are, e.g. by sharing the revenues that are generated by a partner by using the API.

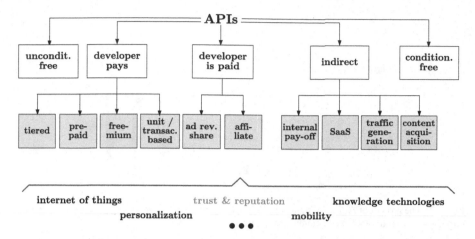

Fig. 4.6 Some early business models related to APIs (derived from [16]) with the main current drivers of their evolution (internet of things, personalization, trust and reputation, mobility, knowledge technologies)

- When a developer is paid, there are two basic variants. The API provider pays the developer based on successful market penetration of the API through the developer's services, or the developer becomes a so-called affiliate partner. There are a few variants of being an affiliate partner. Most often a cost per action payment is offered, where the developer is paid for some sort of action realized by the API (e.g. collection of e-mail addresses). Another variant is the cost per click, which is a self-explanatory kind of payment. The last variant is the referral model. By providing a referral to a provider's API services, the referral model can be a one-time variant, or based on sharing a recurring revenue.

In addition to the above models there are indirect models, which are a very interesting category and comprise the following sub-categories:

- Internally paid-off model is sub-category where a company succeeds, by deploying an API, to internally improve its operations and services.
- Content acquisition sub-category is that one where a partner can directly feed valuable information through the API into its services or information systems.
- The next sub-category is an API that serves for increasing the generated traffic to a company's site or store.
- The last possibility is a rather well-known one: it is called software as a service option (SaaS), which is internal variant of the external ones mentioned above, focused on traffic generation.

Today, the business models structure related to APIs and presented in Fig. 4.6 are rapidly evolving. The main drivers behind this evolution are the internet of things, mobility support, personalization with contextualisation, knowledge technologies, and trust and reputation services.

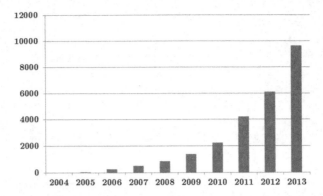

Fig. 4.7 The growth of APIs (the figures used in the figure are those regarding yearly-averages on http://www.programmableweb.com/api-research)

What kind of API will be used (or provided) for a certain trust and reputation management service is dependent primarily on a particular organisation's strategy and related business model. Only secondarily do other specific factors come into play that range from the organisation's actual status to current market situations. Nevertheless, APIs should be considered primarily from the strategic perspective, and secondarily from an operational perspective (for more details the reader is referred to [16]).

*   *   *

Although APIs were discussed in the last section of this chapter, their importance does not rank anywhere near last. On the contrary, APIs are among the most important issues in this chapter when it comes to large-scale deployment of computational trust and reputation management systems. The growth of APIs as shown in Fig. 4.7 speaks for itself.

References

1. S. Allamaraju, *RESTful Web Services Cookbook* (O'Reilly, Sebastopol, 2010)
2. R. Alnemr, C. Meinel, From reputation models and systems to reputation ontologies, in *Trust Management V: 5th IFIP WG 11.11 International Conference, IFIPTM 2011*, Copenhagen, June 29 – July 1, 2011. Proceedings, ed. by I. Wakeman, E. Gudes, C.D. Jensen, J. Crampton (Springer, Berlin, 2011), pp. 98–116
3. D.A. Basin, P. Schaller, M. Schläpfer, *Applied Information Security - A Hands-on Approach* (Springer, Berlin, 2011)
4. T. Berners-Lee, R.T. Fielding, L. Masinter, Uniform resource identifier (URI): generic syntax. Technical Report RFC 3986, IETF (2005)
5. P.V. Biron, A. Malhotra, Xml schema part 2: datatypes, 2nd edn. Technical Report 2, World Wide Web Consortium (2004)

6. B. Boss, The xml data model. web resource. Last Accessed 24 Sept 2016
7. T. Bray, J. Paoli, C.M. Sperberg-McQueen, E. Maler, F. Yergeau, Extensible markup language (xml) 1.0 (5th edn.). Technical Report 5, World Wide Web Consortium (2008)
8. D. Brickley, R.V. Guha, Rdf vocabulary description language 1.0: Rdf schema. W3c recommendation, World Wide Web Consortium, February (2004)
9. S. Casare, J. Sichman, Towards a functional ontology of reputation, in *Proceedings of the Fourth International Joint Conference on Autonomous Agents and Multiagent Systems*, AAMAS '05, New York, NY (ACM, New York, 2005), pp. 505–511
10. R. Chinnici, J.-J. Moreau, A. Ryman, S. Weerawarana, Web services description language (wsdl). Technical Report REC-wsdl20-20070626, Part 1, W3C Consortium (2007)
11. D.E. Comer, *Computer Networks and Internets*, 6th edn. (Prentice Hall Press, Upper Saddle River, NJ, 2014)
12. J. Euzenat, P. Shvaiko, *Ontology Matching*. (Springer, New York, Secaucus, NJ, 2007)
13. D.C. Fallside, P. Walmsley, Xml schema part 0: primer, 2nd edn. Technical Report 0, World Wide Web Consortium (2004)?
14. R.T. Fielding, *Architectural styles and the design of network-based software architectures*. PhD thesis, University of California, Irvine (2000). AAI9980887
15. M. Gudgin, M. Hadley, N. Mendelsohn, J.-J. Moreau, H. Frystyk-Nielsen, Soap version 1.2 part 1: messaging framework. World Wide Web Consortium, Recommendation REC-soap12-part1-20030624, June (2003)
16. D. Jacobson, G. Brail, D. Woods, *APIs: A Strategy Guide* (O'Reilly Media Inc., Sebastopol, 2011)
17. O. Lassila, R.R. Swick, Resource description framework model and syntax specification. W3c recommendation, W3C, Feb (1999)
18. Y. Liu, Y.L. Sun, Anomaly detection in feedback-based reputation systems through temporal and correlation analysis, in *SocialCom/PASSAT*, ed. by A.K. Elmagarmid, D. Agrawal (IEEE Computer Society, New York, 2010), pp. 65–72
19. Y. Liu, Y.L. Sun, Securing digital reputation in online social media [applications corner]. IEEE Signal Process. Mag. **31**(1), 149–155 (2014)
20. D. McComb, *Semantics in Business Systems* The Savvy Manager's Guides (Morgan Kaufmann, Burlington, 2003)
21. H. Mousa, S. Ben-Mokhtar, O. Hasan, O. Younes, M. Hadhoud, L. Brunie, Trust management and reputation systems in mobile participatory sensing applications: a survey. Comput. Netw. **90**, 49–73 (2015)
22. N.F. Noy, D.L. McGuinness, Ontology development 101: a guide to creating your first ontology. Online (2001)
23. P. Resnick, R. Zeckhauser, Trust among strangers in Internet transactions: Empirical analysis of eBay's reputation system, in *The Economics of the Internet and E-Commerce*, ed. by M.R. Baye. Advances in Applied Microeconomics, vol. 11 (Elsevier Science, Amsterdam, 2002), pp. 127–157
24. G. Schreiber, M. Dean, Owl - web ontology language reference. W3c recommendation, W3C (2004)
25. K. Schwaber, M. Beedle, *Agile Software Development with Scrum*, 1st edn. (Prentice Hall PTR, Upper Saddle River, NJ, 2001)
26. Y. Sun, Y. Liu, Security of online reputation systems: the evolution of attacks and defenses. IEEE Signal Process. Mag. **29**(2), 87–97 (2012)
27. P. Tan, M. Steinbach, V. Kumar, *Introduction to Data Mining*, 1st edn. (Addison-Wesley Longman Publishing Co., Inc., Boston, MA, 2005)
28. A.S. Tanenbaum, D. Wetherall, *Computer Networks*, 5th edn. (Pearson Prentice Hall, Upper Saddle River, 2011)
29. H.S. Thompson, D. Beech, M Maloney, N. Mendelsohn, Xml schema part 1: structures, 2nd edn. Technical Report 1, World Wide Web Consortium (2004)
30. D. Trček, *Managing Information Systems Security and Privacy* (Springer, Heidelberg, 2006)
31. E. van der Vlist, *Xml Schema*, 1st edn. (O'Reilly Media Inc., Sebastopol, 2002)

32. World Wide Web Consortium, Simple object access protocol (soap). Technical Report TR 20030624, Parts 0, 1 and 2, W3C Consortium (2003)
33. L. Yu, *Introduction to the Semantic Web and Semantic Web Services* (CRC Press, Boca Raton, 2007)
34. Y. Zhao, (ed.), *R and Data Mining* (Academic, New York, 2013)

Chapter 5
Anticipated Uses of the Presented Tools

Do not stand in a place of danger trusting in a miracle.
(Arabian proverb)

Trust and reputation management systems are already deployed in various areas ranging from assessing services and products to peer-to-peer networking applications. But technology aimed at one particular area of application often finds its way to wider acceptance in other areas. Notable examples include space technology discoveries and their applications in numerous areas of our everyday life.

Trust and reputation management technologies will likely do the same. One such area that comes to mind is their application to simulations in economics, for the reasons given in the first chapters of this book. Another possible and more surprising application area would be in conflict management and peace research.

Conflict management research starts with the identification of agents (individuals) driven by goals that are based on their interests and beliefs. These agents then form new aggregate structures like groups, societies and states, which can be treated as newly emerged entities. All of these entities are in interactions with one another and with a hard to predict (or unpredictable) environment. This results in numerous feed-back loops that lead to complex systems emerging in a bottom-up manner. Consequently, in order to simulate such systems a bottom up approach method is needed that can model their nature. One such option is provided by artificial agents.

Starting with a peaceful setting, entities coexist in a collaborative ecosystem where they, in principle, trust one another to a certain degree. During this phase conflict precursory events may start to form for various reasons. Examples include possible tangible gains, ethnic tensions, etc. These precursory events are followed by conflict emergence, and once emerged, the conflict escalation phase follows. After a certain period of time, which depends on the nature of the conflict and other contextual factors, the observed structure enters into a conflict resolution phase. When (and if) the conflict resolution phase is successfully managed, peace enforcing factors are implemented, which lead to peace keeping factors that finally end up in a peace-preserving continuum.

© The Author(s) 2018
D. Trček, *Trust and Reputation Management Systems*,
SpringerBriefs in Information Systems, DOI 10.1007/978-3-319-62374-0_5

From the emergence of conflict pre-cursory events to conflict culmination and its final resolution many scenarios are possible. But one common thread in the background of these scenarios is the erosion of trust. During conflict escalation trust erosion is taking place, while the closer to resolution a conflict is, the stronger its (re)formation is.

By using agents this section demonstrates how a benevolent society can evolve into a state where extreme trust assessments can be observed, which then form the basis for conflict. Intuitively, negative extreme positions are not something that a wise leader with a focus on productive cooperation would stimulate. Therefore tools to deal with such cases are needed, and we will demonstrate how a principle, which will be referred to as *Just mess with a mass*, can help.

Suppose that an observed population consists of 120 agents, and that these agents are governed by QAD operators (see Chap. 3 for definitions). The initial setting is as follows: All agents are undecided about one another, 45% of them are governed by an extreme optimist assessment, 45% are governed by an extreme pessimistic assessment, while the remaining 10% are assessment hoping. Let us observe what happens with this population after 35 simulations, where each simulation takes 100 steps, and where in each simulation step a randomly chosen 5% of agents randomly change their operators. New operators are selected with equal probability among extreme optimist, extreme pessimist and assessment hoping operators. After running this setting, the cumulative histogram shown in Fig. 5.1, run A, is obtained.

This result of the simulation is worrisome. Clear extremists' wings have emerged and the question is how could this society be driven to a more desirable state with fewer tensions. Assuming that we can more easily affect operators than the initial values of operands (which likely have a minor influence on the outcomes

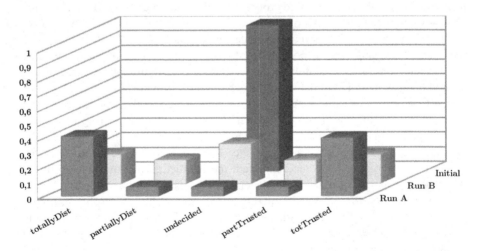

Fig. 5.1 Normalised cumulative distributions of trust values (the situation after run A is in the *first row*, after run B is in the *second row*, while the initial situation is in the *third row*)

as operators), let us try to find a strategy to drive the community towards a more desirable state.

Starting with the same benevolent setting as above in run A, we will now actively interact (in each step) with 25% of randomly chosen agents and try to convince them to change their current assessment operators to whatever the new operators may be (this is what *Just mess with a mass* principle is about). The described intervention is equivalent to a setup where, in each iteration, 25% randomly chosen agents randomly adopt a new operator among existing ones (i.e. a new operator is chosen by a randomly chosen agent with an equal probability among all seven possible operators). The outcome of this situation is given in Fig. 5.1, run B.

The new result is considerably better and it represents a more favourable outcome. Assuming that total distrust means no cooperation, the non-cooperative population has been reduced by approx. 50%. Although the number of partially distrusted operands has increased, these assessments reflect more openness to communication than totally distrusted assessments (and, in the case of negotiations, better grounds for successful negotiations). Moreover, the total number of assessments with a negative connotation, i.e. totally and partially distrusted assessments, is smaller than in the first case. Similarly, the number of those that are not likely candidates for the emergence of conflicts (undecided, partially trusted and totally trusted) has increased as well. The second setting also exhibits visibly less extremist positions and it is therefore less likely to lead to an escalation of conflicts.

To finalize the analysis of the presented cases, the exact average values and the corresponding standard deviations have to be given (TD stands for totally distrusted, PD for partially distrusted, U for undecided, PT for partially trusted and TT for totally trusted):

TD	PD	U	PT	TT	
run A					
5923.34	936.37	937.94	938.11	5664.23	(average)
647.67	106.47	102.22	113.84	580.48	(std. deviation)
run B					
2914.14	2356.46	3936.26	2326.66	2866.49	(average)
543.73	1201.35	403.46	1247.00	506.93	(std. deviation)

*   *   *

The anticipated uses of trust and reputation management systems will likely largely depend on the internet of things. It is not hard to imagine what powerful tool such simulations could be when being driven by real-time (or close to real-time) data from real environments. And this is exactly what the internet of things will enable in the near future.

Chapter 6
Trust and Reputation Systems: Conclusions

All's well that ends well.
(William Shakespeare)

Trust and reputation are phenomena of great importance in our private, public and professional lives. But they do not affect us only personally, they also apply to social structures, business organisations, and even states. With the growing penetration of e-environments via the ubiquitous digitization of our lives, the ways we deal with trust and reputation are being additionally challenged.

This is where trust and reputation management technologies come in. Simply put, they can be considered a kind of extension of our senses in e-environments. How so? As mentioned at the beginning of this book, these e-environments are changing so rapidly that our capacity to adapt to them is being severely challenged. Furthermore, the signals to discern trust and reputation in e-environments differ from those in ordinary environments, and some signals may even be missing. Trust and reputation management systems play an important role in helping to cope with this situation.

The domain of trust and reputation management systems is still actively evolving. Therefore it should not be surprising that their wider acceptance and further development of more sophisticated implementations have yet to take hold. The good news is that not only trust and reputation models, but also the arsenal of necessary technological building blocks for their implementation is already available and largely standardised. This book starts with a broad presentation of the general concepts of trust and reputation, continues with coverage of the main methods and models of trust and reputation management for e-environments, provides insights into the necessary technological building blocks that are needed for the establishment of these systems, and provides a roadmap for planning and implementing these systems. On top of this, the book anticipates additional applications of such systems that may be hard to imagine from our current perspective.

Can we predict when these systems will become ubiquitous? Probably the best answer is suggested by the following. In the mid-1990s computer networks specialists used to tell jokes like "If we worked and delivered results the way artificial intelligence community does, there would still be no Internet".

© The Author(s) 2018
D. Trček, *Trust and Reputation Management Systems*,
SpringerBriefs in Information Systems, DOI 10.1007/978-3-319-62374-0_6

Now for more than 15 years no one jokes about artificial intelligence anymore. Decades of accumulated research and newly generated knowledge in the this domain are amassing at a stunning rate. Today, artificial intelligence applications in data mining, pattern recognition, fuzzy logic—you name it—are actually running our lives. In many cases these technological artefacts know more about us than we do. Is it any wonder that many well-known and respected individuals are calling for rethinking further development and deployment of these technologies, for fear that they may even engender the lives of human beings?

But such discussions already exceed the scope of this book...

Printed in the United States
By Bookmasters